'Prayer isn't boring, but we can be in the way we ‚  'asy –
talking to someone who is invisible is a ‚ tive
helps, Claire invites us to invest in our pr‚ us
and nudge us towards growth in our know‚
Jeff Lucas, author, speaker and broadcast‚

'Claire has written a fantastic, creative resource ‚ches and individuals alike.
Many of us are not too confident when it come‚ ‚viding interactive prayer activities
within church, but Claire has given ideas as well as practical instructions on how to carry
them out… We all need to be refreshed in God's presence, and sometimes our approach to
spending time with him needs fresh input too – you'll find plenty within the pages of this
book. So go on, delve in!'
Claire Musters, author of *Taking Off the Mask* (Authentic Media, 2017), speaker and editor

'Prayer can be as easy and natural as breathing but most of us will also find it a challenge at
times, struggling to focus, fighting apathy and boredom, fearing silence and the otherness
of God. Claire has given us a great gift in this book – the gift of ideas that will renew flagging
enthusiasm for prayer. Clearly structured, permeated with biblical truth and endlessly
creative, this resource will become a great friend to any involved in planning and leading
communal prayer times and anyone wanting to add colour to their personal prayer lives.'
Jo Swinney, author of *Home: The quest to belong* (Hodder & Stoughton, 2017)

'This is such a timely resource, which helps us explore new ways to stop and receive in the
place of prayer – as individuals and households, as well as in groups. I think the way each
theme is both grounded in God's word and based on practical creative actions opens up
many new opportunities to encounter God – so much needed in our fast-paced world.'
Jane Holloway, National Prayer Director, World Prayer Centre, Birmingham

'As life gets busier and the world more connected, finding ways to take a breath and speak
with God can be challenging. This resource is full of ideas to engage the senses, reflect
on God's word and pray. I hope it captures the hearts and focuses the minds of many
communities, encouraging them to draw closer to God.'
Carla Harding, National Director, 24-7 Prayer Great Britain

'This is a fantastic resource for those exploring reflective prayer… Claire's book offers a
wealth of thoughtful and spiritually uplifting reflections and prayer activities that deepen
relationships with oneself, others and God. The attention to detail and clarity of instruction
makes this excellent resource easy to follow and replicate… A wonderful tool for those on
a spiritual journey in need of encouragement, refreshment and nourishing.'
Mike Down, Growing Younger Schools Project Manager, CofE Birmingham

The Bible Reading Fellowship
15 The Chambers, Vineyard
Abingdon OX14 3FE
brf.org.uk

The Bible Reading Fellowship (BRF) is a Registered Charity (233280)

ISBN 978 0 85746 673 0
First published 2019
10 9 8 7 6 5 4 3 2 1 0
All rights reserved

Acknowledgements
Unless otherwise acknowledged, scripture quotations are from The Holy Bible, New International Version (Anglicised edition) copyright © 1979, 1984, 2011 by Biblica. Used by permission of Hodder & Stoughton Publishers, a Hachette UK company. All rights reserved. 'NIV' is a registered trademark of Biblica. UK trademark number 1448790.

Scripture quotations taken from the New American Standard Bible®, Copyright © 1960, 1962, 1963, 1968, 1971, 1972, 1973, 1975, 1977, 1995 by The Lockman Foundation. Used by permission. (www.Lockman.org)

Extracts from the Authorised Version of the Bible (The King James Bible), the rights in which are vested in the Crown, are reproduced by permission of the Crown's Patentee, Cambridge University Press.

Scripture quotations taken from the Holy Bible, English Standard Version, published by HarperCollins Publishers, © 2001 Crossway Bibles, a division of Good News Publishers. Used by permission. All rights reserved.

New English Translation NET Bible® copyright ©1996–2006 by Biblical Studies Press, L.L.C. www.netbible.com. All rights reserved.

Scripture quotations taken from the Holy Bible, New Living Translation, copyright © 1996, 2004, 2007, 2013. Used by permission of Tyndale House Publishers, Inc., Carol Stream, Illinois 60188. All rights reserved.

God's Word Translation (GW) copyright © 1995 by God's Word to the Nations. Used by permission of Baker Publishing Group.

Every effort has been made to trace and contact copyright owners for material used in this resource. We apologise for any inadvertent omissions or errors, and would ask those concerned to contact us so that full acknowledgement can be made in the future.

A catalogue record for this book is available from the British Library

Printed and bound by TJ International

80 Reflective Prayer Ideas

A creative resource
for church and group use

Claire Daniel

BRF

For my mum.
You began my life with prayer,
when you placed your tiny, premature baby into God's hands.
Thank you for being my constant in every season of life.

Acknowledgements

My thanks to Mike Parsons, Claire Proudman and the BRF team, who have helped with every step on the journey to publication. I'm thankful to have been blessed with the opportunity to create another collection of prayer ideas.

Mum and Charles, thank you for the many ways you love and support us and for going the extra mile to help make the completion of this book possible. Chris and Graham, thank you for your loving support and prayers. We are so blessed to have such wonderful parents/ grandparents to our boys; you mean so much to us all.

My thanks to Paul Tullet, my church family and housegroup – for giving me the space to share my prayer ideas in our worship together, and for your prayers and words of encouragement.

Thank you to all who have prayed for me as I journeyed with this book. Special thanks to Sam S, Becky C, Hannah J, Demelza, Geraldine, Kayla and my APC Prayer ladies. I love how we share life and faith together in a real way. Your friendship is such a blessing.

Amy Boucher Pye, you bless me with your enthusiasm for alternative prayer methods and the gift of your encouraging words. Thank you for writing the Foreword to accompany my reflective prayers.

I am blessed by unexpected friendships of faith forged through social media, with special thanks to Joanna Chee, Kara Lawler and Lillian Gill. We are truly kindred spirits, and your support of my ministry has encouraged me in this writing journey. Thank you to Bonnie Gray and all of the Whispers of Rest book club: my sisters in Christ. It's been a privilege to travel together, exploring rest as God's beloved.

My heartfelt gratitude to all who bought, used or recommended *80 Creative Prayer Ideas*. I pray you've been blessed as you embraced alternative prayer methods and that you find further inspiration to rest and reflect, using the ideas in this resource to meet with God afresh.

Love and thanks to Gary, Ewan and Benjamin – my boys! Thank you to Ewan for your thoughtful help with developing one of the rainbow prayers and to Benji for the sheer joy of testing out the bubble wrap, modelling dough and toy brick prayers with you! To Gary, for being my hero, my best friend and my rock – the adventure continues!

Words alone cannot fully express my gratitude to God – for the journey he has taken with me in writing this book, and the inspiration and strength he blessed me with as I explored prayer and new ways to respond and rest in him. Lord, may those who spend time with you in reflective prayer find rest and new joy, through the words you inspired in me.

Preface

Reflections of God's glory and symbols of his love and grace can be seen in everyday things. Many of the prayer responses included in this book came to me as I went about my daily life, yet suddenly came across something that spoke to me of God and resonated with me about the journey of faith. I find I encounter God very powerfully in the unexpected moments of everyday life, at home, on holiday or when doing seemingly ordinary things, like listening to a song or playing with modelling dough with my toddler.

I love developing creative ideas for reflecting on God's grace, and I am greatly moved by images as well as words. For example, the rainbow ribbon prayer in chapter 5 was inspired by an incredible art installation I saw in Grace Cathedral, San Francisco. These are my responses to God, thoughts that I believe he has dropped into my mind during times of reflection. That is not to say that I spend all day feeling inspired, praying effusively and profusely to God (far from it!). I do, however, believe that it is important in our faith walk to take time out to reflect and pause, to listen to God and to respond.

I have been developing ideas since writing *80 Creative Prayer Ideas* and finding new ways to focus on rest, with a fresh appreciation for the need to replenish our spirits in our busy world. I've recently encountered new ways to meet with God personally and new methods of expressing my faith in creative yet reflective ways, through Bible journalling, prayer-doodling and Christian colouring resources. In writing on reflective prayer, I've been exploring our need to stop, and it's challenged me to consider how we take time to breathe and refocus on our own relationship with God. There is benefit in finding ways to reconnect with him and to rest and reflect, especially in the hectic seasons of life. We need to find activities that renew our souls, giving ourselves permission to pause and make space to meet with God. I hope you can discover ways to do this through contemplative prayer.

I pray that these ideas spark a passion for reflecting, helping you meet with God in new, unexpected ways, as you adapt these prayers to suit your own needs and those of the church or group you share them with. May you encounter God through prayer, reigniting joy in the weary parts of your soul, as you experience hope, listen for his voice and bring your heart to him in fresh or renewed ways.

Contents

Reflecting on our personal walk with God

Foreword

When I opened the email, I was delighted to glimpse a photograph of a large plant bursting with lush leaves and pea pods. Immediately, I guessed that the person who sent the email had attended the BRF *Woman Alive* women's conference I spoke at a couple of months previously. There, during my session, I handed out little wrinkled pea seeds and led the women in a prayer exercise as they held them, asking God to grow our faith during the seasons of our lives.

I read her email, touched by the words:

> I'm now harvesting a small but delicious crop of mangetout. It was the perfect illustration of how something appearing to be dried up and dead can flourish and become productive with the right type of care, so thank you for that. It is a lesson I will try to take into my spiritual life both for myself and others, especially to try not to judge someone by outward appearances but look for the hidden fruitfulness within them.

Even though I knew intellectually that a pea seed could bring forth new life, seeing the photograph of such abundant growth helped me to receive the truth at a deeper level. For I've long prayed that in my writing and speaking, God would give me his seeds to fling widely, that he would be the gardener who will tend them, bringing them to life and fruitfulness. Seeing a physical manifestation of that prayer encouraged me deeply.

And the original pea seed exercise? It was partly inspired by Claire Daniel's *80 Creative Prayer Ideas*, her resource that gathers together engaging ways to help us pray individually or in a group. Now she follows up that wonderful book with 80 more ways of praying not only creatively but reflectively, which I'm delighted to recommend.

Why am I so keen on these types of prayer activities, including them when I speak to groups and in *The Living Cross* (BRF, 2016), the Lent book I wrote on forgiveness? Because they can be a means to encounter God. Not every exercise will touch every person, of course, and some people might approach the activities with some fear and the notion that they aren't creative. But no previous stores of creativity are required – honest! And the benefits will outweigh any niggling hesitation, for the very act of engaging in these exercises involves a level of humility and an openness to receive from God that I believe he honours. Being willing to take part opens space for God to speak to us. He can bring to life what may have been an intellectual concept, as he did for me with the pea pods, or help us get in touch with buried emotions, or shower us with his love.

So I warmly recommend Claire's *80 Reflective Prayer Ideas*, a book that I hope many people will embrace. She provides a variety of ways to engage our senses with themes that are firmly rooted in the Bible as she leads us to reflect on God's word, nature, the church community, our journey of faith and our personal walk with God. She starts each exercise with a passage from the Bible as she helps us ponder its meaning and how its truth might apply to us before leading us into a conversation with God. Feeling the soil in between our fingers while planting seeds or hearing the pop of the bubble wrap or smelling the coffee or tea will help us to enter more fully into the experience of meeting with God, being present and receptive to how he speaks into our lives.

Claire's book is not only for individuals, but will be a wonderful tool for those leading others. For instance, I'm preparing to speak on the theme of living in and for Christ, and am gravitating to her exercises on spiritual transformation. As she says, even as a caterpillar changes to a butterfly, so are we changed to be more like Christ.

I'm grateful for how Claire helps us to foster an encounter with God through the living Christ and the empowering Spirit. May God use *80 Reflective Prayer Ideas* to plant and grow many seeds that will bear fruit in his name.

Amy Boucher Pye

Introduction

Prayer is a vital part of our Christian journey, yet finding the words to express our hopes, hurts, failings and joy is not always easy. The ideas in this book provide ways to bring our prayers to God through practical yet reflective responses, using visual prompts, creative actions, Bible verses and suggested prayers.

The prayer responses are designed to be personal, reflective acts of worship. They do not necessarily require any great artistic ability but do allow you to express your faith creatively. They are prompts for your individual response to God, a different way of pouring out the things that are on your heart, through prayer. You may want to write longer responses or do some journalling in a separate notepad as you read each prayer, or you may choose to spend time in quiet contemplation, write a single word or draw something as you pray.

Many of the prayers deliberately engage our senses, as well as give opportunity to respond with our heart and words. Using our hands and tactile experiences, looking at images or listening to music can help us experience a sensory style of worship and a deeper connection with God than words alone. I wanted to create prayers that are fun, challenging and even messy in places, just like our faith journey. I also wanted to make them accessible to those who find traditional prayer difficult, those who have additional needs and those with vision or hearing impairments.

In my ministry, I have had the opportunity to create and use many of these ideas at conferences, prayer workshops, women's weekends or in my own church. I've also had fun getting my children involved in having a go at some of them as I developed the ideas, like the bubble wrap, white board and modelling dough prayers. I can tell you that the sound of bubble wrap popping beneath stamping feet of various sizes, as you give your worries over to God, is indeed hugely cathartic!

Prayer is for all ages and stages of our faith journey. These reflections can be used by individuals, church congregations and small groups, and for setting up prayer events or all-age worship. They can also be used as a basis for prayer rooms or quiet spaces, in churches, retreat venues, conferences, schools or youth clubs, or in family prayer time, children's ministry or holiday club activities. It is powerful to use a reflective idea as a whole group or congregational response, while still making an individual prayer response. It can be an amazing experience to respond together as a body of believers. Equally, you may want to use this book as part of your personal devotional time and quietly reflect on the prayers.

The prayer station ideas set out in each chapter are ready to use and can be the basis of an 'instruction sheet' for each station, or they can be used as a starting point, the springboard for your own creative response to God. Prayer is very individual, and God will lead you to pray in ways I couldn't write for you; but my hope is that, as you read the words I have included, you will rest in God's presence. I pray that God will speak to you as you pause to reflect and use these ideas as a guide for the path of prayer that you need to take with God, that you might hear from him and open your heart to all he has for you.

Getting ready

There are a few practical things you may want to consider as you prepare to set up reflective prayer stations, particularly if you are new to this type of worship response. These will vary depending on the space you are using and the type of activities you choose to provide but there are some general areas worth thinking about as you get started and plan for an event.

Venue/furniture

What changes will you need to make to the layout of the furniture to set up stations? What sort of lighting do you have and do you need to add in any extra lights to create atmosphere? Some of the stations you are setting up may need tables and chairs and good lighting; others may need soft furnishings, such as cushions or beanbags, and more relaxed lighting.

Electricals/AV use and safety considerations

Do you need additional lamps or equipment to play music or display slideshows? It may seem obvious but in preparing your event, you will need to ensure that you have these prayer stations set up near power sockets in your venue and that all equipment is set up and maintained to meet health-and-safety regulations, avoid trip hazards from wires, and so on. If you are using real candles in any of the stations, be aware of fire hazards and put into place precautions, following the fire regulations for your venue.

Handwashing/kitchen availability

If you are planning to do responses that generate mess or involve food, do you have suitable kitchen and handwashing facilities? It is worth considering positioning stations so that those who need access to clean water or handwashing are near a kitchen or sink. In some situations, a bowl of warm washing-up water that can be changed at intervals or even packs of hand wipes are sufficient. You will also need to ensure you have plenty of kitchen towel to deal with any spillages. Use protective table coverings and even sheets for the floor if you anticipate lots of mess, particularly if your venue has carpets or is used for other purposes.

Resources

It's great to have some general craft kit for prayer stations. Basics like paper, card, glue, scissors, pens in good working order and a whole range of other craft equipment can be useful. Things like plastic bowls, durable table coverings and washing-up bowls are also worth purchasing. There are lots of online retailers that provide good-quality craft resources in bulk if you need larger quantities at reasonable costs, so do shop around.

Bibles and Bible verse cards

Many of the prayer station ideas use Bibles to reflect on specific scripture or cards printed with Bible verses to take away, in addition to the 'Bible reflection' verse for each idea. It is good to have a selection of different translations available. Cards with Bible verses can be printed at home and cut into different shapes. You can also buy ready-made ones.

General prayer ideas

Some prayer responses can be used for a variety of themes and with materials different from those suggested. I encourage you to adapt ideas from the chapters to other topics, get creative with resources you have and add your own ideas! Sometimes having six or more stations is good, depending on the event and venue size, or you may just want to use an idea as a single response as a congregation, or as a prayer response in a service or group meeting. These are some methods of reflecting that can be tailored to suit various prayer topics:

- Gratitude list/happy list
- Bible journalling
- Colouring (for all ages)
- Modelling clay/dough
- Rest-and-reflect area
- Written journalling
- Sticky notes
- Prayer doodling
- Graffiti wall
- Food response, e.g. icing biscuits
- Pebbles
- Candles
- Bible verse cards to take away
- Prayer walks/labyrinths
- Reflecting on nature
- Music to inspire reflection
- Visual prayer aids: photographs or images (printed or shown on a screen)

Reflecting on the Bible

1
Reflections on the Psalms

Where my help comes from: Psalm 121

Prayer focus

To look to God, our helper in times of need, the creator of the world. Using the grandeur and splendour of a mountain, to reflect on the awesome power of God, who can move mountains yet is also our refuge and comforter.

Bible reflection

I lift up my eyes to the mountains – where does my help come from? My help comes from the Lord, the Maker of heaven and earth.

PSALM 121:1–2

What I need

- Large green, brown or white cardboard sheet
- A4 card or paper, cut into small mountain shapes
- Marker pen
- Scissors
- Glue (if cutting out shape)
- Pens

Either cut out and construct a large mountain landscape from the cardboard, or draw a large mountain on to the white cardboard with the marker pen. Print or write the words of Psalm 121:1–2 on to small mountain-shaped cards to take away.

Reflect

When we spend time looking at the natural world around us, the sight of a mountain or range of hills can evoke feelings of awe at their sheer size and towering presence in the landscape. They can also help us remember the strength of our creator God, who made all things yet also cares about each of us and is our source of help when we face 'mountains' in life.

Pray

Take some time to look at the large mountain in front of you. Consider the significance of this image in your life. Perhaps call to mind incredible scenery you have seen on your travels and bring prayers of thanksgiving to God for the beauty of the created world. Reflect on those things in your life that may feel utterly insurmountable, like a huge mountain. Remember that when we put our faith and trust in God, he can move mountains – nothing is impossible for God. Lay these before God in prayer, as you read the verses from Psalm 121, giving thanks to him, your comfort and the source of help in times of need. If there are times you have neglected to lift your eyes to the Lord and you need to look to him again in awe and worship, do this as you look at the mountain. If you would like to respond by writing down your prayers or words of thanksgiving, add these to the mountain as you believe afresh that the God who created the splendour of a mountain also knows about all that you face and wants to comfort you. Take a small mountain verse-card home as a reminder to look to God and give all your 'mountains' to him.

Fearfully and wonderfully made: Psalm 139

Prayer focus

To reflect on the wonder of being created by God. Though we may feel insignificant, God knitted together our very being and knows us from before we came into existence. God has a plan and purpose for our growth, and a hand in our development at every stage of life and faith.

Bible reflection

> For you created my inmost being; you knit me together in my mother's womb. I praise you because I am fearfully and wonderfully made; your works are wonderful, I know that full well.
>
> PSALM 139:13–14

What I need

- Magazines with pictures of people of different ages
- Photographs of babies, ultrasound scans and perhaps also of other ages and stages of life, from children to the elderly (either personal copies or printed from the internet)
- Scissors
- Glue
- Large sheet of paper or cardboard
- Marker pen
- Pens

Print or write the words of Psalm 139:13–14 in the centre of the large sheet of paper or cardboard in big, bold lettering, leaving plenty of space around it.

Reflect

Sometimes we may feel that our faith is embryonic, that we have far to go in our understanding and development as a Christian. Or it can feel as if we are in a phase of life where our faith is growing as fast as a child, with big changes happening as we journey with God. If you are honest, you might have been a Christian for a long time and feel rather 'aged' in your faith – wise perhaps, but in need of a renewal of the energy of youth and vitality of early faith. God is with us in whatever season we find ourselves in on our faith journey. You are fearfully and wonderfully made.

Pray

Look through the magazines and photographs and spend a few moments cutting out some pictures as you consider the theme of human growth and development. Choose some images to stick around the verse, creating a prayer collage of different ages and stages of life. As you do this, begin to bring your faith journey to God, be open with him in prayer about the season you are in. Give thanks for the miracle of life and that God has made us all unique and wonderful, with individual talents and purpose. Consider ways you have grown in maturity in your walk with the Lord. If you feel your faith is in need of revitalising or that growth has slowed or even ceased, bring this before God, asking for a renewal of strength and opportunities to focus on your faith development. Reflect on ways you can rediscover this vitality, perhaps through rereading significant Bible verses or starting a new Bible study or devotional and sharing where you are with others in your church or family, as you look to grow together in faith.

The wonder of creation: Psalm 8

Prayer focus

To give thanks to God for his power and majesty in creating the world, even setting the stars in place. To respond to the awesomeness of God the creator. To reflect on our responsibilities as custodians of the world God created for us.

Bible reflection

When I consider your heavens, the work of your fingers, the moon and the stars, which you have set in place, what is mankind that you are mindful of them, human beings that you care for them?

PSALM 8:3–4

What I need

- Blue card or length of blue material
- Silver card or paper
- Scissors
- Glue sticks
- Pens
- Pins or double-sided tape (if using material)
- Metallic star stickers

Cut out star shapes from the silver card or paper and put out the material or card, the pens, the star stickers and whatever you are using to fix the stars in place.

Reflect

When we see the stars and consider the infinite nature of space and all that God has created, we can feel a sense of awe. It can also be humbling to reflect on the knowledge that the God who placed the stars in the sky also created each of us. He made you and placed you on the earth for a purpose, and he made us all guardians of the world we inhabit.

Pray

The moon and stars are so incredible to see, shining in the darkest of nights. Psalm 8 is a reflection on the majesty of God's creation, in all its greatness, and an outpouring in praise of the creator God, the maker of heaven and earth. It also acknowledges our responsibility and role to care for the world. Look at the blue paper before you, a wide expanse to represent the heavens. Take some time to reflect on the enormity of the universe and give thanks to God who placed the stars in the sky, yet also knows you, loves you and created you. Write a prayer on the back of a silver star. Fix your star on to the sky, thanking God for the world and praying for a fresh appreciation of its beauty and the ways we can care for it. Take with you a small metallic star sticker, and place it somewhere you will see as a reminder that the hands of God that flung stars into space also took time to create you. He has a plan for your life, however insignificant you may feel.

The Lord is my rock: Psalm 18

Prayer focus

To use words of hope to inspire and encourage. To reflect on God, our rock in whom we can take refuge, a stronghold in times of trouble and uncertainty.

Bible reflection

> The Lord is my rock, my fortress and my deliverer; my God is my rock, in whom I take refuge, my shield and the horn of my salvation, my stronghold.
> PSALM 18:2

What I need

- Pebbles
- Permanent marker pen
- Decorative table cloth

Use the permanent marker pen to write a word of inspiration on each pebble. Choose words you feel are appropriate, such as 'strength', 'hope', 'grace', 'mercy', 'peace' and 'light'.

Reflect

Take some time to look at the words written on the pebbles – words of affirmation and inspiration. These words mean different, significant things to each of us and may bring to mind different circumstances, struggles or concerns. They are words of hope and strength, and the pebbles themselves can remind us of the unchanging and solid rock that is God, our refuge and deliverer.

Pray

Select a pebble. Look at the word written on it as you hold it in your hands. Use this word to guide your prayers. Or perhaps you may ask God to speak to you afresh through the word written on the pebble, bringing your worries and cares to him, the rock of your salvation.

You might want to reflect on several of the pebbles in this way. Take time to use these simple but powerful words to inspire your reflections and prayers as you hold on to the words of hope that God, our rock and strength, gives.

When you are ready, choose a pebble with a particularly significant word on it to keep. Take this home and place it somewhere where you will see it – perhaps your bedside table, desk or kitchen window ledge – to remind you of your prayers and to continue to inspire you.

2
The Lord's Prayer

Hallowed be your name

Prayer focus

To praise and worship the name of the Lord. To reflect with reverence and awe on the names of God, responding with prayers of adoration.

Bible reflection

> Therefore, since we are receiving a kingdom that cannot be shaken, let us be thankful, and so worship God acceptably with reverence and awe.
> HEBREWS 12:28

What I need

- Large sheet of cardboard
- Marker pen (or print an outline of the word 'LORD' in large font size)
- Coloured pens or pencils
- Other (optional) craft items for decorating, e.g. paint, glitter, stickers, ink stamps

On the cardboard sheet, write the word 'LORD' in big, bold letter outline, with space inside each letter to write, or stick on the printed outline. Put this out with the pens and (optional) decorations.

Reflect

'Hallowed' is not a word we use often, apart from when we recite the Lord's Prayer or perhaps when we refer to our favourite sports venue as 'hallowed ground'. It is defined as 'to be honoured as holy', to be revered as sacred. It is also a verb, 'to hallow', something that we therefore should do, not just say. How often do we repeat this well-known prayer, yet not entirely consider the wording? Take some time to think about this and the importance of the names of God that are used in the Bible. How do you refer to God? Do you use his name with reverence, and honour it as holy?

Pray

Consider the names of God that we might use in different seasons and circumstances – Father, Lord, Creator, God, Yahweh. What does it mean to you to call on the name of the Lord? Take some time to reflect on the names of God that come to mind and acknowledge times when you do not call on his name or 'hallow' his name in your daily life. Consider the name, 'Lord', that is before you in big, bold letters. Write within the outlined letters the name or names of God that you use. When you call upon him, do you refer to him as 'Lord', 'Heavenly Father', 'Creator' or some other name? Write as many as you like or perhaps write a prayer or some other words of worship and adoration. Spend some time prayerfully considering the words you have written, the ways that you speak to and about God in your daily life. You may want to pray a prayer of thanksgiving or acknowledge those times when you do not give the reverence due to the name above all names.

Your will be done

Prayer focus

To surrender our lives into God's hands, asking for his guidance and leading, for his will not ours to be done. To ask God to guide our actions and to know his will for our lives.

Bible reflection

> I have been crucified with Christ; and it is no longer I who live, but Christ lives in me; and the life which I now live in the flesh I live by faith in the Son of God, who loved me and gave himself up for me.
> GALATIANS 2:20 (NASB)

What I need

- Large sheet of cardboard
- Tissue paper or thin paper sheets (various colours)
- Marker pen
- Scissors
- Glue sticks

Draw a large outline of flat, open hands on the cardboard and cut them out. Cut out little pieces of tissue paper and place these out ready with the hands and glue sticks.

Reflect

It is sometimes hard to accept that our plans and ideas may not actually be the best thing for us, or that there may be a better plan for our life. We strive so often to be independent and self-sufficient. This can be a good thing, of course – God does not want us to have no independence – but the world often prizes self-reliance above relying on the support of others. Not needing to consult anyone for guidance, including God, is celebrated as positive. However, when it comes to our relationship with God, we are called to surrender our will and our ways, entrusting ourselves into his hands, seeking his guidance above our own plans at times, to truly follow his will and purpose for our life.

Pray

Consider occasions in your daily life when you do not seek God or commit your actions and decisions into his hands. These might be seemingly small and insignificant instances or bigger life-decisions. Take a piece of tissue paper and, as you hold it in your hand and then gently scrunch it into a ball, bring these situations to God in prayer. Perhaps there are parts of your life or your behaviour that you struggle to give over to God, where relinquishing control is hard. Ask God to help you entrust these into his hands. You may want to say, as you respond in the quietness of your heart, 'Lord, your will be done.' We so often repeat this phrase in the Lord's Prayer, yet perhaps do not always consider the meaning of it or act in the knowledge of this declaration of surrender to our heavenly Father. When you feel ready, glue the tissue paper on to the hands, surrendering all those things into God's hands and trusting in his will and purpose for your life.

Give us today our daily bread

Prayer focus

To reflect and give thanks for the ways God provides for all our needs, satisfying our hunger, both spiritual and physical. To pray for those who do not know the spiritual nourishment God can give and for those who have physical needs for daily bread.

Bible reflection

> And Jesus said unto them, I am the bread of life: he that cometh to me shall never hunger; and he that believeth on me shall never thirst.
> JOHN 6:35 (KJV)

What I need

- Sliced bread
- Edible-ink pens or writing icing tubes in various colours
- Paper plates

Reflect

In the Lord's Prayer, we ask that God might 'give us today our daily bread' (Matthew 6:11). We petition the Lord that he might provide for our needs, satisfying our hunger with food that sustains us. But 'daily bread' has a deeper significance when we reflect on Jesus' words in John 6:35 that those who believe in him will be nourished both physically and spiritually. Consider ways that God and your relationship with Jesus bring you a fullness of life that bread alone cannot supply. How does knowing Jesus sustain you daily and continually?

Pray

Take a slice of bread. Before you begin to write on it, take a moment to look at this symbol of provision; bread is a staple food that can fill us up and abate our hunger temporarily. Think about all the things God provides you with – food to eat and his word that feeds our spiritual needs. You may want to simply write 'Thank you' on the bread, or you may choose to write a longer prayer. Or you may want to write, 'Jesus, bread of life', as an affirmation that through Jesus, God provided a way that we would never go hungry in a spiritual sense. Take some time to pray for those in our world who have a real need for even the most basic of food, that we might do all we can to relieve this hunger. Pray for those you know who do not yet know the sustaining love of God. When you eat the bread, give thanks to God for nutritional food but also for the ways your faith helps you grow and gives you energy and life.

As we forgive those who sin against us

Prayer focus

To let go of hurt and to replace it with love. To acknowledge that we need God's help to forgive. To learn to forgive as God forgives us, yet acknowledging that this can take time and repeated prayer.

Bible reflection

'And when you stand praying, if you hold anything against anyone, forgive them, so that your Father in heaven may forgive you your sins.'
MARK 11:25

What I need

- Whiteboard
- Red whiteboard pens
- Whiteboard eraser
- Chairs

Set out the whiteboard, pens and eraser ready, with the chairs nearby.

Reflect

Forgiving others can be a long process, and it can be painful and difficult. Yet God calls us to forgive, as he forgives us. We may find it hard to forget the hurts caused by others, yet in order to live in true freedom, we need to ask God to help us let go of these – release our anger, bitterness or disappointment – and help us move on. Take some time to bring to God those things others have said or done to you that you know you still carry and struggle to forgive. Quietly and honestly share these with God.

Pray

Take a red whiteboard pen and colour a patch of the whiteboard; as you do this, bring to mind those things others have said or done that made you feel angry or upset. Put the pen down and take a seat. While you sit, with your eyes closed if you feel more comfortable, make your hands into fists, as you think of those words or deeds that cause you to feel anger towards someone. When you feel ready, move your hands into a prayer pose, palms together, as you pray for the strength to truly release the hurt to God. Finally, form a heart shape with your thumbs and index fingers to show that you want to try to replace the anger towards others with the love that God shows you, then open your hands and reach outwards as a symbol that you are releasing all you have prayed over to God.

When you feel ready, stand and walk over to the whiteboard. Wipe away the red mark of anger that you added and draw in its place a heart, to represent your commitment to forgive those who have wronged you, as God forgives you.

3
Chosen for great things

Trusting in God's timing

Prayer focus

To trust in God's timing when prayers seem to go unanswered. To pray for patience and faith in God's plan for our lives.

Bible reflection

> Now the Lord was gracious to Sarah as he had said, and the Lord did for Sarah what he had promised. Sarah became pregnant and bore a son to Abraham in his old age, at the very time God had promised him.
> GENESIS 21:1–2

What I need

- Sand egg timers

Reflect

Sarah and Abraham were chosen to establish a nation, yet for so long it seemed as if their prayer went unanswered. In the same way, we might bring our hopes to God many times and find it hard to trust in his timing. Like Sarah, we may doubt that he is fulfilling his promise, yet if we are patient we will see the fruition of the plans that God has for us, grown from seeds of faith planted and nurtured by prayer over many years. We can become disheartened and impatient as we wait. Sarah doubted, yet remained faithful, and God's promise was fulfilled. Are there some things you have been praying for repeatedly or over a very long time, yet God does not seem to have heard your prayers or answered? Do you struggle with impatience or doubt as you wait for God's timing?

Pray

Trusting that God knows what is best for us is often really challenging. Like Sarah, there may be times when we doubt God has heard our prayers. When he seems silent and many years have passed, the idea of him fulfilling a promise long-held or answering our prayer may seem laughable. Bring your doubts and feelings of impatience to God, turning over your frustrations to God, as you turn over the sand-filled egg timer. Watch as the sand silently slides very slowly through the timer, using this to guide your prayers. Time can seem to move more slowly when we are waiting for an answer or for a change in our circumstances. Trust afresh God's perfect timing as you watch the sand drain through and reflect on the story of Sarah and Abraham.

Listening for God's voice

Prayer focus

No matter how young or old we are in our faith, God wants to speak to us. To take time to listen for God's voice and respond.

Bible reflection

> The Lord came and stood there, calling as at the other times, 'Samuel! Samuel!' Then Samuel said, 'Speak, for your servant is listening.'
> 1 SAMUEL 3:10

What I need

- Large sheet of cardboard
- Marker pen
- Pens
- Scissors (if cutting out the ear shape)

Draw the outline of a large ear on the cardboard with the marker pen. You may want to then cut it out. Put pens out ready.

Reflect

God wants to speak to us, if we will just take time to listen for his voice. When we call out to him, he may not always respond straight away but, like Samuel, we can learn to recognise God's voice. We might hear an audible message from God or sense him speak through scripture or the words of others when we are open to hear from him. Samuel was young, but God chose to reveal his plans and spoke directly to him. However young in our faith or unimportant we feel, God has things he wants to say to us and wants us to listen and respond. Think of those times in your life when you have heard from God. Perhaps he spoke actual words into your heart or mind, or you felt a strong sense of his presence. Have there been significant times when you knew God was speaking to you directly through scripture, as a verse leapt out to you, or through the lyrics of a worship song or the significant words of someone else? Do you need to tune back in to listening for God's voice, taking time to pause, ready to hear and respond?

Pray

Before you respond, spend some moments in quiet, asking God to help you to pause and to listen patiently for his voice, both now and in your daily life. Pray that you might be open to hear from him. Give thanks for the times God has already spoken into your life. Pray for more willingness to hear from God and acknowledge those ways you have stopped listening for his voice, in the busyness of life. Bring these feelings to God and write a response on the cardboard ear. Close by praying to have ears open to hear, an open heart to receive. Be confident and trust that, just like Samuel, the Lord can speak to each of us, in different ways, regardless of our age or whether we feel 'worthy'. As you finish, resolve to continue listening for God's voice and discerning when God is speaking to you through others, through signs, through scripture or audibly.

Overcoming our giants

Prayer focus

God can help us overcome our giants. However young we are, in years or in faith, or however ill-equipped we feel, God gives us all we need to face our fears and fulfil his plan.

Bible reflection

> David said to the Philistine, 'You come against me with sword and spear and javelin, but I come against you in the name of the Lord Almighty, the God of the armies of Israel, whom you have defied.'
>
> 1 SAMUEL 17:45

What I need

- Pebbles of various sizes
- Grey or white paper or card, cut into pebble shapes
- Scissors
- Pens

Set out the pebbles, pens and pre-cut pebble shapes.

Reflect

Cairns are used as markers on a journey, to remember a path already taken or as a memorial to someone or a significant event. They remind us of all we have learned as we travel back along a pathway and are a chance to reflect on the journey we have been on and the obstacles we have overcome. These piles of stones, which feature in the Bible, are a reminder that as you return along a path, you return changed by the journey and the things it taught you. Our experiences of difficult times in life alter who we are, shape us and help us grow. David overcame a giant with a small pebble and his trust in the almighty God. We too can overcome those things that seem giant and stack up against us in life when we put our faith and trust in God's strength.

Pray

Take a pebble and hold it in your hand. Bring to mind those things that you are facing that feel like giants. Think about those circumstances that seem impossible and too huge to defeat in your own strength. Place your pebble down and carefully stack more on top, to make a pile. As you place each one, pray about what it represents to you – health worries, broken relationships, family or work situations, or perhaps something else. However insurmountable these giants feel, trust them to God, as you pray.

Consider those 'giants' you have already overcome in the past, giving thanks to God for those times when he has resourced you to face a challenge that felt way beyond your human abilities.

Leave your pebbles stacked and take a small pebble-shaped card. You may want to write on it the Bible reference from this prayer or another word or prayer. Take this 'pebble' with you as a reminder of God, your rock and strength when you face 'giants'.

For such a time as this

Prayer focus

Like Esther, we are chosen 'for such a time as this' – we are where we are for a reason. To pray for the strength not to remain silent about injustice and to make a difference where we are.

Bible reflection

'For if you remain silent at this time, relief and deliverance for the Jews will arise from another place, but you and your father's family will perish. And who knows but that you have come to your royal position for such a time as this?'
ESTHER 4:14

What I need

- Craft jewels or sequins
- Large sheet of purple or similar-coloured card or material
- Other coloured card or paper, cut into small crown shapes
- Glue or double-sided tape

On the small crown shapes, print or write the words 'For such a time as this' and the Bible reference and glue on a small craft jewel. Put these out along with the length of material or card and glue or sticky tape.

Reflect

We do not have to be royalty to have an impact in the world; we can all make a difference in the place we find ourselves, if we bravely use our voice for good. God can give us direction as we seek opportunities to speak up and discernment to know when it is our time to speak out against injustices. Think of times when it would be easier to stay silent when you see injustice in the workplace, at church or in your community. It takes bravery to speak out and wisdom to know the right words and timing. But if not you, then who? If not now, when? Perhaps God has placed you exactly where you are to speak against injustices like bullying or unfair treatment. Even if you feel unimportant or insignificant, you can make a difference! Though you may not have a 'royal position' of influence, trust that God has placed you where you need to be, to advocate for others and share his heart of indignation for injustice.

Pray

It can take boldness and preparation to be ready to fulfil the role God has for you. Esther was called to act but had to go through a process of making ready first. Timing was key; to act rashly was dangerous, yet she knew she could not remain silent. Even when she was ready, Esther took a huge risk in speaking out, knowing it was for the greater good of her people. Bring your prayers to God, for the bravery to speak out in situations where you see injustice and for the discernment to know those who need help and the right time to speak. Pray as you add a jewel to the 'royal robe' that God will prepare you and help you know how you can make a difference in your community. Ask him to show you ways you can make an impact, perhaps just by speaking quietly to someone, or offering kind words or practical support. How might God be using you in the place you are right now? For such a time as this is right now! Take away a crown-shaped verse card with a jewel on as a reminder of your prayers, an encouragement to be brave and a prompt to embrace opportunities to speak out for others, as Queen Esther did.

4
God, our refuge in the storm

God, our anchor

Prayer focus

To give our storms and trials to God and to trust that he is our anchor, holding us firm when the waves of life threaten to engulf us.

Bible reflection

> We have this hope as an anchor for the soul, firm and secure.
> HEBREWS 6:19

What I need

- Large sheet of plain cardboard
- Blue paper or card
- Marker pen
- Scissors
- Pens
- Adhesive putty (e.g. BluTack) or double-sided tape

Draw a large anchor outline on the sheet of cardboard with the marker pen and cut it out (optional). Cut small wave shapes from the blue paper. Put out the adhesive putty or double-sided tape.

Reflect

Sometimes, certain seasons or experiences we go through seem like a stormy sea and we feel jostled by the waves. Perhaps you are facing times of ill-health, worries or loss that have left you adrift in a sea of struggles, with no sign of the shore. God is the anchor for our weary souls, a hope that remains firm. His love reaches out to hold us firmly, sure when all else is uncertain, when troubles surround us like relentless waves. Reflect on the Bible passage from Hebrews. God is our anchor, a place where our soul can rest secure, our source of hope when all around us or within us is in turmoil.

Pray

Pick up a wave shape and consider all the 'waves' that are surrounding you at this time, the things that are stopping the sea of your life being calm and peaceful. You may want to write a word or prayer on the wave. Seek God in prayer, asking for his love to anchor you, to bring a stillness to your soul, despite the storms you are encountering. Remember those times of upheaval and struggle in the past and give thanks to God that he has been present and helped you hold fast to him in times of trouble.

Believe afresh as you look at the anchor that, however stormy life gets, God is with you. He is a stronghold in the storm. Attach your wave to the anchor as your prayer response, giving your troubles and uncertainties into God's care. You can be sure that he will be an anchor of hope and strength with you in the midst of even the roughest seas of life.

God, our place of shelter

Prayer focus

God's love surrounds and upholds us. His comforting arms are a shelter and refuge from the storms of life.

Bible reflection

> God is our refuge and strength, an ever-present help in trouble.
> PSALM 46:1

What I need

- Blue shawls or blankets or lengths of blue material
- Comfortable chairs, beanbags or cushions

Reflect

Life can be stormy at times, and we can feel knocked off our feet by a barrage of different things; wave after wave of worries or concerns can be relentless and rob us of our peace. We may forget to come to God, the source of our peace and shelter, in the middle of all that life is throwing at us. Yet this is when we need to take time to stop, rest in his presence and ask him to surround us with his comfort. When life gets too much, we need to come back once more into the embrace of our loving Father God. Take some time to rest right now, find a comfortable place to sit and gently wrap a shawl around you.

Pray

Take your time, as you sit with the blanket or shawl wrapped around you, to breathe. Give yourself permission to be still, close your eyes if you wish and breathe slowly, in and out. Focus on the feel of the material surrounding you, like the arms of God encircling you in a loving embrace.

While you spend some time just resting in God's presence, pray in whatever way you feel led. You may just want to be silent, thank him for his presence or pour out your concerns about all that is currently overwhelming you. As you breathe gently in and slowly out, release your worries to God with each exhaled breath, asking him to be your shelter and place of safety.

Only when you feel ready, slowly unwrap the shawl from around you. Leave your concerns with God and take with you the feelings of calm and peace you felt, wrapped in God's embrace.

Peace in the midst of the storm

Prayer focus

God doesn't always calm the storm, but we can still know peace, because he is with us even in the midst of stormy times.

Bible reflection

'Peace I leave with you; my peace I give you. I do not give to you as the world gives. Do not let your hearts be troubled and do not be afraid.'
JOHN 14:27

What I need

- White wax candles or wax crayons
- A4 white thick paper or card
- Blue paint
- Water in water pots or jam jars
- Paintbrushes
- Tablecloth

Put out some paint and water, along with the paper, wax candles or crayons and paintbrushes. Cover your table with the tablecloth if necessary.

Reflect

It is sometimes hard to feel truly at peace when we feel weighed down by the turmoil of life. We can become consumed by the circumstances and worries crowding our mind, causing us to feel far from peaceful. What is troubling your heart today? What storms of fear or anxiety are causing you to feel adrift in a turbulent sea? God wants you to know peace despite your circumstances because he is with you, even when troubles come, wave after wave. Meditate on John 14:27 and invite God to fill your heart with peace, the peace that only he can bring. Ask God to comfort and help you overcome your fears as you give them over to him.

Pray

Use a wax candle or crayon to write the word 'Peace' in large letters in the centre of the paper provided. It is barely visible, yet it is there. There may be times in your life when you barely notice God at work in you, walking with you daily. Now take a paintbrush and paint a blue wash over the page. Bring to God the waves of worry that crowd your mind and disturb your peace, as you make waves with each brush stroke across the page. Watch as the wax resists the paint and the word 'Peace' is clearly seen in the centre. Ask God to reveal to you again his peace within the stormy waves of life. Take your picture with you as a reminder that God can fill us with a peace that is stronger than any storms we face. Continue to pray that God would give you a clear sense of his peace filling your heart when the waves of life seek to overwhelm.

Calming the storm within us

Prayer focus

God doesn't always take away the troubles of life, but helps us through them by calming the storm within us. To learn to hold on to God when the storms don't end, trusting he will sustain us until they subside.

Bible reflection

'Have I not commanded you? Be strong and courageous. Do not be frightened, and do not be dismayed, for the Lord your God is with you wherever you go.'
JOSHUA 1:9 (ESV)

What I need

- CD or streamed sound effects of crashing and calm, lapping waves
- CD player or smartphone/laptop
- Headphones (if required)
- Comfortable chairs
- A4 cardboard
- Scissors

Print the words of the verse (Joshua 1:9) multiple times on to the A4 cardboard, then cut into smaller cards to take away (optional). Set up chairs near your CD player or smartphone/laptop and get the music ready to use. Have headphones to use if the noise will disturb other people.

Reflect

God can calm a storm, yet sometimes rather than stopping the waves, he calms us with his presence, giving us an inner peace in the midst of the challenges we face. When the storms continue for a season, we need to lean into God as our place of safety. In trusting God to lead us through the waves of life, there can be much to learn as we rely on God's strength. What storms are you facing? Do you need to stop trying to solve the problems that rage around you like crashing waves? Instead, choose to invite God to guide you through the storms, knowing he can uphold you and trusting there are calmer seas to come.

Pray

Put on the headphones or press play on the sound recording. Sit comfortably, closing your eyes if it helps you to focus, and listen to the sound of crashing waves. Immerse yourself in the sound, praying as you feel led about any storms you are facing. Take time to come to God in the midst of any turbulent situations you are experiencing, asking him to be a peaceful presence. If the sound changes to a calmer sea, with gently lapping waves, pray that God might lead you to a place of calm within, even as the storms of life continue, knowing that he is with you. Ask God for patience to endure the storms and for an understanding of what he wants you to learn as you go through them, with him as a constant presence. Give thanks for those times when God guided you through stormy times in the past or calmed the storms within you.

When you have finished your time of reflection, take a verse card away, as a reminder that God is with you in every storm of life.

Reflecting on nature

5
Rainbow prayers

God's rainbow promise

Prayer focus

To reflect on how clouds and sunshine need to be present for a rainbow to appear. To thank God for his promises fulfilled and to trust in the rainbows yet to come.

Bible reflection

> 'Whenever the rainbow appears in the clouds, I will see it and remember the everlasting covenant between God and all living creatures of every kind on the earth.'
> GENESIS 9:16

What I need

- Large sheet of paper or cardboard
- Various sheets of paper or card in the colours of the rainbow
- Scissors
- Glue stick
- Pens or pencils

On the large sheet of paper or cardboard, create a rainbow scene by cutting and pasting large arches and sun and storm-cloud shapes from the coloured paper/card.

Reflect

Rainbows are an incredible sight, a wonder of nature yet also an image of hope. Bright colours shine forth as light mixes with the rain of a storm, creating a symbol of God's covenant with Noah, made for all generations to come. Though we know the science behind rainbows, as Christians they are significant as a reflection of God's promise fulfilled. Rainbows exist when there is light within a storm, a beautiful image of hope shining despite the storm clouds that have gathered. What does the sight of a rainbow mean to you personally? Take time to reflect on the covenant from God it represents, those promises God has fulfilled in your life or perhaps the 'rainbows' you are still praying for and hoping to see.

Pray

A rainbow can fill the sky, spanning great distances like God's far-reaching love that extends down to us. You may want to write prayers along the arches of the rainbow as you reflect on the hope we have in God's promises. Or you may choose to write a prayer on the sun or storm clouds in the picture. If you feel there are clouds in your life, write a prayer in the cloud shape, asking God to be with you. You may want to write a prayer of thanksgiving for answered prayers or blessings on the sunshine. The rainbow can represent prayers answered, or for you it might symbolise the hope of a promise yet to be fulfilled. Use the whole picture before you to help you reflect on the light that can follow a season of storms or darkness in life, as the rainbow symbolises God's promise of hope fulfilled.

Rainbow of grace

Prayer focus

To thank God for his promises, his grace and the hope we find in him. To see our prayers going up to God and the promises of his grace flowing down to us.

Bible reflection

Your love, Lord, reaches to the heavens, your faithfulness to the skies.
PSALM 36:5

What I need

- Medium-thickness silk ribbons in the colours of the rainbow
- Embroidery frame hoop, or wire (e.g. wire coat hanger) shaped into a circle
- Scissors
- Pens that will write on ribbon

Cut lengths of ribbon.

Reflect

God's grace and love flow freely down to us when we seek him and bring our prayers to him, like a rainbow reaching down to earth, bringing light. A rainbow can remind us of God's promises and answers to our prayers extending down to us, as our prayers flow upwards to God, the reflection of our faith and trust in his promises to us. Light reflects and refracts through a rainbow, making its colours shine – a symbol of grace and hope renewed – but they are all different. Some rainbows are clear, full, vibrant arches, while others are barely visible; they are all still rainbows. Sometimes, God's promises or answers to prayer may be hard to see clearly among the clouds of life. Yet his grace and love still flow down, bringing hope and light, however faint the rainbow of his promise might seem.

Pray

Choose a ribbon from the lengths provided, perhaps a colour that holds a special significance for you or one that you feel drawn to. Take a moment to appreciate the texture of the ribbon, the smoothness of it, giving thanks to God for ways he has smoothed situations in your life. Alternatively, ask him to bring a shine back to places in your life or the lives of others where a fresh touch of God's grace is needed. Write a prayer along the ribbon: words of thanks for the ways God has fulfilled his promises or you have experienced his grace or hope. Pour out your heart to him. Write just a few words or the names of anyone you want to lift to God, or write a longer prayer, filling the length of the ribbon with your personal words to God. When you have finished, you may want to take some time to pause and listen, to hold the ribbon as you pray expectantly for the grace you want God to pour down. Acknowledge that prayer, like a rainbow, is God's way of communicating down to you, as well as a way for you to send your requests up to him. When you are ready, tie your ribbon on to the hoop provided. When suspended, the ribbons catch the light, shimmering with colours, creating a free-flowing rainbow of hope and a visual representation of so many prayers lifted heavenward, and of God's grace and love flowing down.

A rainbow: God's hope in dark times

Prayer focus

The light of God's promises can shine through even the darkest times. To see hope shining through a rainbow, with the dark surrounding it unable to overcome it.

Bible reflection

> The Lord is my light and my salvation – whom shall I fear? The Lord is the stronghold of my life – of whom shall I be afraid?
> PSALM 27:1

What I need

- Tissue paper in the colours of the rainbow, cut into strips or squares
- Black construction paper or card
- Light box or window
- Scissors
- Adhesive putty (e.g. BluTack)
- Glue
- List of Bible scriptures about God as light, etc. or printed cards with verses to take away (optional)
- Bibles
- Paper
- Pens

Cut the black construction paper into window frame shapes, perhaps arched at the top to resemble a stained glass window outline, with open space left in the middle to fill with the overlaid tissue paper 'glass'.

Reflect

God's promises in scripture can be a great source of encouragement when we encounter difficult and dark times. There are many verses in the Bible that offer comfort for times of struggle and speak of God's love and light. We can put our hope in the light of his love that casts out fear and trust that he has a plan, whatever our current circumstances. Are you facing situations where darkness seems to be winning and hope seems to be a dim and fragile light? Do you need to look to God and his promises afresh and trust that he is stronger than any fear the dark times hold? Are there particular verses of scripture that help when shadows surround you, to rediscover or hold on to the hope and light of God's love?

Pray

Reflect on the dark window frame shape in front of you – the imposing colour and all it might represent to you in your life or as you think of others or the world. Contrast these thoughts with the feelings inspired in you by the brightly coloured tissue paper, almost translucent yet vibrant in colour; fragile in texture, compared to the dark frame, yet beautiful. Choose some pieces to add into the window, overlapping them as you glue them together, creating a range of colours. Bring your thoughts to God in prayer as you respond creatively. Share with him your hopes, any darkness you face or the need for light in your life or that of others. Pray for our world, where so much seems overshadowed by despair and where darkness seems to hold dominion. When you have created your tissue paper stained-glass window, give thanks for God's light that shines as you place it on a window or light box, symbolising your prayer for God's light to shine in every place and circumstance.

Look up a favourite verse on light, or use the verse cards and suggestions to meditate upon. You may want to write some of these on to the paper provided or take a printed verse card away with you.

Rainbow of prayer for all

Prayer focus

To bring our prayers for the world, other people and ourselves to God, reflecting on the promise God made to all.

Bible reflection

> 'I have set my rainbow in the clouds, and it will be the sign of the covenant between me and the earth. Whenever I bring clouds over the earth and the rainbow appears in the clouds, I will remember my covenant between me and you and all living creatures of every kind.'
> GENESIS 9:13–15

What I need

- Large sheet of white or plain cardboard
- Small scraps of material, plain or patterned, in the seven colours of the rainbow: red, orange, yellow, green, blue, indigo and violet
- Glue sticks or PVA glue
- Scissors
- Small bowls or containers
- Marker pens

On the large cardboard sheet, draw the outline of wide rainbow arches with a black marker pen. Write the colour name in each band of the rainbow (to be covered over by the scraps). Pre-cut scrap pieces of the different colours of material. Place each colour into a different bowl or container and put out glue. You may want to add a Bible verse to the collage sheet or just cut out the rainbow afterwards.

Reflect

There are so many things we might feel called to pray for; the many needs of the world, our community, ourselves and those close to us can leave us unsure where to start. The enormity and number of situations we want to bring to God can fill our hearts with heaviness and burden our minds. Take some time to consider all the things that weigh heavy on your thinking and lay them before God. Meditate upon the image of a rainbow – a symbol of hope for all the world, yet also a message for you and your community, and a reminder that God's power can overcome darkness and bring light to all.

Pray

Look at the scraps of material. Use the following rainbow colours to bring your reflections into focused prayer topics: red for thanksgiving; orange for forgiveness; yellow for our church and community; green for hope; blue for the world; indigo for people we know; and violet for ourselves. The rainbow of colours is as diverse as the needs and prayers they will represent. Take some time to feel the texture of the scraps or enjoy their bright colours as you pray, choosing a scrap of coloured material and reflecting on the people or situations it represents for you. Bring these to God as you hold the piece, then glue it on to the corresponding coloured arch, as a symbol of giving your prayers to God and trusting that he can send light and hope into any and all situations. Take time to reflect and respond using as many of the colours as you like, unburdening yourself of any concerns you carry in each of these areas of need, as you give them prayerfully to God. The scraps will build up a colourful collage of prayers and a visual reminder of the rainbow as a symbol of God's promises and hope.

6
Growing where we are planted

Rooted in God

Prayer focus

To reflect on the roots of a tree that firmly anchor it, digging deep, unseen beneath the ground to keep it from falling. To stay rooted in God.

Bible reflection

> But blessed is the one who trusts in the Lord, whose confidence is in him. They will be like a tree planted by the water that sends out its roots by the stream.
> JEREMIAH 17:7–8

What I need

- Large sheet of cardboard or paper
- Marker pens
- Pens, pencils or felt-tip pens

Draw a large tree outline on the large sheet of paper or cardboard, with roots reaching down and spreading out. Ensure the roots are wide enough to fit written names or prayers inside them.

Reflect

Consider the strength and support a tree gets from its roots, a wide spreading network that goes deep into the soil. Unseen below the ground, this network enables the tree to stand firm, withstanding the elements. A tree can be shaken, yet it takes a lot to uproot one entirely. When we root our lives firmly in God, he provides the strength, nourishment and network of support we need to remain strong, grow deeper and spread wider in our faith. Perhaps you are feeling shaken or even uprooted in the current season of your faith journey and need to be planted afresh into the rich soil of God. Because of its unseen roots, a tree stands firm. In the same way, God can keep us grounded, as the source of our strength. Consider ways you could spread wider or deeper roots of faith through prayer, taking time to refocus on the network of support that connects you to God.

Pray

Write your name or a prayer in the root network of the large tree outline, giving thanks for the way God has kept you rooted in him. Or ask for God's help to grow a deeper connection with him, planting fresh or wider-reaching faith roots. Pray for those in your network, who stand with you and help keep you rooted in your faith, those who have mentored you in your faith journey, helping you connect with God and develop a firm grounding in him. Ask God to inspire you with ways to stay grounded in him, reflecting on those things that nourish your spiritual soil and enrich your faith journey, such as Bible reading, quiet time with God or spending time with other Christians. Look at the other names or prayers around yours in the root network; we are all connected by our desire to be rooted in God and need to support each other. One root could never hold up a tree; a collection of them are needed – just as we are stronger when we share our faith journey with others. You may want to ask others to pray with you, to support you in rediscovering your roots in God or to help you grow deeper and wider in the ground of your faith.

Waiting for growth

Prayer focus

To pray for patience when a situation seems dead and prayers seem unanswered. To trust God's timing and thank him for times when new life and hope have flowered in your life.

Bible reflection

> For in this hope we were saved. But hope that is seen is no hope at all. Who hopes for what they already have? But if we hope for what we do not yet have, we wait for it patiently.
> ROMANS 8:24–25

What I need

- Flower bulbs
- Soil
- Small plant pots
- Small trowels or other suitable tools
- Table cloth or protective covering

Reflect

Bulbs remain unseen below the ground, yet they are germinating, waiting for the right time to sprout with new life. In the same way, God's timing is perfect and he is at work in the seasons of waiting; his plans for your life are not dormant. When it seems the Lord is silent, he has not forgotten you; he has heard your prayers – the answer is coming. You will grow from the process of patience and prayer even though the 'flower' that appears may not be quite the one you expected. Trust that God has a plan and that when the time is right, the answer will become clear, like a green shoot finally bursting through the surface of the seemingly dead ground, a display of new life and hope.

Pray

Respond in prayer as you plant a bulb. While you prepare the flower pot, adding soil, ask that God might receive your prayers. Add your chosen bulb, a symbol of latent hope, seemingly dormant yet containing the potential to flower. It just needs time and the right conditions for it to flourish. Pray for patience in those areas of your work, family life or ministry where there seems to be no visible growth. As you cover the bulb with soil, commit those things to God, bedding in your prayers. Ask God to show you how to nurture the situation and give it the right conditions to grow, trusting in his timing. Bring to God your desire to grow in your faith, and be honest about those areas in which you find it hard to be patient and believe that he is at work for your good. Take your planted bulb home with you. Care for it with water and by placing it in a sunny location, and wait patiently for it to grow. Use each stage of its development as a fresh opportunity to pray, as you trust God's timing in your life and wait for a shoot to appear and for the flower in the pot to eventually bloom.

Beauty instead of ashes

Prayer focus

To give thanks for new life and the fresh start we can have because of Christ's sacrifice, the hope of the cross and the beauty of nature.

Bible reflection

> … to bestow on them a crown of beauty instead of ashes, the oil of joy instead of mourning, and a garment of praise instead of a spirit of despair. They will be called oaks of righteousness, a planting of the Lord for the display of his splendour.
>
> ISAIAH 61:3

What I need

- Large wooden or cardboard cross
- Silk or real flowers
- Floristry wire or strong twine
- Scissors

Wrap the wire or twine around the whole cross, spaced at intervals. Make sure it's loose enough for the flower stems to be slipped underneath but tight enough to hold them secure.

Reflect

When Jesus gave up his life upon the cross, darkness descended and death appeared to have had the last word. But through his amazing resurrection in glory, Jesus brought life everlasting. God's eternal rescue plan was fulfilled so we might know light in dark times, a fresh start and the hope of life after death. Beauty and blessings can replace mourning; we can rise from ashes. The cross is no longer a symbol of death and torture but represents Jesus' victory over sin and death, giving us a new life and fresh start. Flowers and the beauty of nature also reflect the hope of new beginnings, when beautiful flowers grow from soil that seemed unable to sustain life. Reflect on the hope we can find in Jesus, even in the most barren or desolate circumstances.

Pray

Take a flower and reflect on the beauty of it, its freshness and vibrancy. Give thanks to our creator God for the beauty of nature, the colours, scent and visual joy of flowers in bloom. Yet flowers grow in soil, which is dark and far from beautiful, and which spends much of the year appearing to sustain no life. Perhaps you are travelling through a season of loss, illness, worry or uncertainty, when all seems dark and hopeless. Bring to God in prayer those things that burden you. Lay them at the foot of the cross, knowing that as you do this with an open heart you can come to God and he accepts you and loves you just as you are. Jesus died for you, that you might know new life with God. The Saviour took the sins of the world upon his shoulders, bearing the punishment for us all, that we might live in freedom. Place a flower on to the cross as your response, remembering the new life and hope that is yours through Jesus' sacrifice.

Unfolding like a flower

Prayer focus

To pray for God's help to reveal our gifts, that we might flourish with his strength and have the courage to use our gifts.

Bible reflection

> For the Spirit God gave us does not make us timid, but gives us power, love and self-discipline.
> 2 TIMOTHY 1:7

What I need

- Paper in various pastel colours
- Scissors
- Pens
- Washing-up bowl or similar
- Water
- Protective table covering

Draw and cut out paper flowers with four large petals around a small centre circle, so that each petal can be folded inwards separately on top of each other. Fill the washing-up bowl about half way.

Reflect

We all have unique gifts and talents that God can use for his glory. It takes courage to step out and reveal our talents, but God can help us. He created each uniquely beautiful flower to bloom in their own special way and time. In the same way, the Lord created you and delights in seeing you grow and bloom as you share your gifts. Are there things you are good at that you are hesitant to display in your workplace, church or community? Perhaps you have an interest in playing an instrument, singing, speaking or offering to help with children's ministry or prayer support? Do you need God to give you the confidence to believe in your own abilities, your beauty and your significance?

Pray

Take a paper flower shape and hold it as you consider the ways you need God's help for your God-given talents to bloom and to use them confidently in ways only you can. Write a word or prayer on each petal. In the centre, you may want to write the name of God as you ask him to be your source of courage as you seek to grow and blossom in your gifts. Or leave the flower blank and simply hold it as you pray in the quietness of your heart. Fold each petal over the centre, overlapping each other. Carefully place the flat, folded-up flower on the surface of the water. Pray for God to help you step out in your gifting or help you discover new ways your faith can bloom, as you watch the paper flower slowly unfold. God's Holy Spirit can help us to be bold in our faith; pray for a fresh touch from his Holy Spirit to give you the strength to overcome any nerves at taking steps of faith. As the whole flower shape is revealed, know that God will uphold you as your gifts unfold slowly, like the water supporting the paper flower. It can take time to flourish but, if we trust God, he will help us to bloom.

7
The vine and the branches

Vine and branches prayer

Prayer focus

To commit afresh to staying connected to God, remaining close to the vine, the source of our strength and the spiritual nourishment we need to grow in faith.

Bible reflection

'I am the vine; you are the branches. If you remain in me and I in you, you will bear much fruit; apart from me you can do nothing.'
JOHN 15:5

What I need

- Flexible thin wire or green garden twine
- Purple and shades of green paper
- Sticky tape or masking tape
- Pens

Cut out paper shapes of vine leaves and bunches of purple grapes. Cut a large length of wire or twine and hang this up or attach it to a wall to be the vine. You may want to fix each shape on to the wire or twine or provide sticky tape.

Reflect

The branches and leaves of a vine can spread far, but in order to flourish they have to remain connected to the vine, nourished by its roots. However strong a branch may become, if it is cut from the vine it will wither and die, ceasing to bear fruit. Jesus uses the powerful image of a vine to convey our need to stay close to God, to be in relationship with him through Jesus, in order to grow and bear fruit in our lives. Are there ways in which you have become less reliant on God? Perhaps there are small yet significant ways you can reconnect to him, through prayer and a conscious seeking of his strength to help you bear fruit in your walk of faith?

Pray

Take some time to reflect as you select a paper vine leaf or bunch of grapes. Sometimes, vines can become too widespread and need to be cut back to remain healthy. Are there ways you have branched out away from God? Are there areas of your life that need pruning by God, or things that prevent you from receiving nourishment from God and staying near to him? Consider the ways you would like to be more connected to God in your daily life or ways you need his help to step out in faith and bear fruit. Write a prayer on the shape you have selected: perhaps words of thanksgiving or a request for more of the nourishment that you need from God, the source of all strength. You may want to bring your confession to God for those ways in which you have knowingly or unconsciously broken away from him and need to connect once more. Respond by fixing your leaf or fruit on to the vine, as a symbol of your resolve to stay in relationship with God in your daily life and your desire to bear fruit, committing your prayers to God.

Bearing good fruit

Prayer focus

To pray to be more intentional in displaying the good fruit that we can bear, through kind words and actions.

Bible reflection

'For there is no good tree which produces bad fruit, nor, on the other hand, a bad tree which produces good fruit. For each tree is known by its own fruit.'
LUKE 6:43–44 (NASB)

What I need

- Brown and various brightly coloured card
- Scissors
- Pens
- Small plastic bin/compost bin

Cut out shapes of fruit (e.g. apples, oranges, bananas), some from the brightly coloured card and some from the brown card.

Reflect

When picking fresh fruit, we select those pieces that look the most appealing. Ripe, colourful fruit that tastes sweet and delicious is chosen; any that are mouldy, taste bitter or have gone bad are unfit to eat and rejected. We all have things in our life that do not reflect the good fruit that God gives us, the things we try to demonstrate to the world in our words and deeds. We need to get rid of attitudes or behaviours that produce bad fruit, making us bitter and preventing us from being fruitful for God. What fruit do you produce in your life? Do your actions and words show the world that you live by faith and demonstrate God's love to others? Do you try to be 'sweet' to others or are your words and treatment of those around you sometimes rather bitter?

Pray

Take a colourful fruit shape and reflect on the verses from Luke's gospel. Write down the things you want to be known for, on this piece of fruit that is bright and delicious-looking. You might want to write a prayer about the 'fruit of the Spirit' you are thankful for or the ones you'd like to bear more of, such as peace, patience, goodness or gentleness. Or perhaps say a prayer of rejoicing for the good fruit you've seen grow in your community or changes God has helped you to make in your own words or actions. Next, take some time to reflect on those ways you do not show the 'sweetness' of God's love, the actions or situations where, if you are honest, you sometimes bear bad fruit. Pray this through with God and add these negative feelings or times you act in ways you shouldn't on to a brown fruit shape. Pray that God might help you cut these out of your life and bear only good fruit. Place this bad fruit into the compost bin provided as your commitment to rid yourself of the bad fruit in your life, with God's grace. Take your good fruit with you as a reminder to bear good fruit, to use kind words, and to show God's love and 'sweetness'.

Thanksgiving tree

Prayer focus

To consider the many wonderful gifts God has given us, the things we are thankful for and how we might share God's love with others.

Bible reflection

> Thanks be to God for his inexpressible gift!
> 2 CORINTHIANS 9:15 (ESV)

What I need

- Branches or wire shaped into a tree
- Vase or similar to hold the tree (if using branches)
- Colourful gift tags or cut-out card shapes
- Ribbon or twine

Set up a 'tree' of branches in the vase and put out gift tags (attach the ribbon or twine to them) and pens.

Reflect

When we pray, we can often find ourselves so burdened with concerns for others, for our personal health or for family needs that we forget to begin by praising God, giving thanks for our blessings. Though God wants us to carry every burden to him in prayer, sharing all that makes our heart heavy, we also have much to thank him for. Consider your blessings, the joys in your life. Whatever your current circumstances, lay these down and call to mind the ways God has answered your prayers and all you want to praise him for. Reflect upon the gifts and talents he has helped you develop or the people and events that have blessed your life.

Pray

Despite the many hardships of life, our blessings are numerous, like buds sprouting forth from a tree branch. Select a gift tag. Write on it a prayer of thanksgiving for the gifts God has blessed you with or a prayer asking for a spiritual gift to help you share the gift of God's love and salvation with others. You might want to spend some moments quietly praying, thanking God for the gifts he has blessed you with and for his love and faithfulness. You can write a prayer or a single word to describe what you are thankful for. Or perhaps use this as a chance to reflect on a gift from God that you would like to share with others – for example, joy, hope or peace. Meditate on how you can share God's love and blessings with others and reflect thanksgiving in your daily life.

Hang your gift tag on a branch as part of a tree full of prayers of thanksgiving, blooming with colour, proclaiming God's faithfulness and representing hope and answered prayers.

Filling our cup

Prayer focus

To pray for refreshment for our body and spirit. To thank God for the spiritual nourishment he provides through the Holy Spirit.

Bible reflection

> May the God of hope fill you with all joy and peace as you trust in him, so that you may overflow with hope by the power of the Holy Spirit.
> ROMANS 15:13

What I need

- Grape juice
- Grapes
- Bowl
- Jug
- Disposable cups
- Tablecloth

Fill the jug with grape juice and put out bowls of grapes and cups.

Reflect

There are times when we feel we are running on empty, surviving but not thriving, in our daily life and in our walk with God. If we are honest, we often become so busy that we forget to take time to stop and draw strength from the Lord, who can fill our 'cup' and provide for every need. Physical thirst can be temporarily satisfied by a drink, but we can only find true and lasting refreshment from God's Spirit poured out for us, through Jesus' sacrifice. Do you need to take time to ask God to fill your 'cup' again, so that you can find refreshment from the vine and strength for the journey?

Pray

Pray as you pour the juice into a cup, reflecting on Jesus' blood poured out for us. Ask God to refill your spiritual 'cup' with the strength you need and to refresh your faith. Meditate as you drink the grape juice on the fruity taste and our need for spiritual refreshment, which Jesus offers. Take some time to pray, giving thanks to God for the spiritual refreshment he gives when we ask him to fill us with his strength and the power of the Holy Spirit. Eat some grapes, savouring the burst of refreshing juice as you do this, and meditating on the way God provides nourishment for our weary souls, giving us the fruit of his Holy Spirit to help us in our faith. While you enjoy the fruit of the vine, bring to God any emptiness you are feeling and be honest about the ways you may have neglected to stay connected to him. Ask that you would know refreshment of body and spirit to serve him and stay close to the source of your strength. When, at other times, you drink fruit juice or enjoy the sweetness of grapes or other fruit, recall your prayers and ask God to continue to fill your 'cup' with all you need, trusting he can sustain you.

8
Transformation: caterpillars and butterflies

Caterpillar Christian

Prayer focus

To pray against fear of failure and the things that hold us back, not comparing our abilities to those of others.

Bible reflection

Do not conform to the pattern of this world, but be transformed by the renewing of your mind. Then you will be able to test and approve what God's will is – his good, pleasing and perfect will.

ROMANS 12:2

What I need

- Wooden craft sticks
- Craft pom-poms
- PVA glue
- A4 construction paper/coloured paper or cardboard
- Scissors
- Googly eyes
- Pens

Reflect

Change can be unsettling. However, when we trust our lives into God's hands, we can be confident that our creator can help us transform. Are there areas of change in your life that you are resisting? Have you felt God prompting you to make a change that seems impossible to achieve? Do you compare yourself to others? We need to trust that God can help us transform and focus on the gifts we have, not those of other people. Caterpillars can transform only into the specific butterfly they were born to be; we too can only seek our personal transformation. Your transformation is in God's hands. Trust him with your gifts and believe he can help you do the impossible.

Pray

Take a wooden craft stick. Glue some coloured pom-poms along it and add googly eyes. As you do so, pray about the things that seem beyond or out of reach of your abilities. There may be some things you are reluctant to do. Your caterpillar is uniquely designed, just like you. God does not want us to be a carbon copy of others or to conform to the behaviours of the world. We are made in his image. Reflect on the verse from Romans 12 as you make your caterpillar, praying through with God the ways you feel you want to be transformed in your thinking or actions. Pray for the confidence to be the person God created you to be. Ask God to help you stand firm in your faith, and be strong enough to embrace change with his help.

If you want to go further, take a piece of A4 paper and draw around your hands one at a time, with your thumbs together in the middle. The resulting outline resembles a butterfly. Take some time to think about those changes that seem impossible and give this from your hands into the hands of God, who can do more than we can imagine. Place your caterpillar into the centre of the hand 'wings' where the thumbs join to make the butterfly body. Use this as a symbol of committing your prayers for transformation and the confidence to fly in your own way to God.

Chrysalis days

Prayer focus

Change can be slow and painful, and it might seem like nothing is happening. But, just like the transformation within a chrysalis, God is changing you in small stages.

Bible reflection

> [You] have put on the new self, which is being renewed in knowledge in the image of its Creator.
> COLOSSIANS 3:10

What I need

- Large sheet of brown cardboard or paper
- Scissors
- Pens

Cut out a large, oval chrysalis shape from the cardboard/paper. Put out pens ready.

Reflect

A caterpillar can grow rapidly, ready to begin its metamorphosis into a butterfly, yet the time it spends changing inside the chrysalis can be a number of weeks, up to a year for some species. Unseen, radical transformation slowly occurs within this unassuming silken casing. How incredible is it that inside such a simple, unattractive cocoon, a caterpillar can entirely change its shape? In slow, deliberate stages, it alters until it is ready to emerge as the beautiful butterfly it always contained the potential to be.

Do you believe that there are things about you that can never be changed, because of long-held ideas about yourself, your abilities or negative things others have said to you? Do you feel impatient for transformation? Have you been praying for change in your life, yet nothing seems to be progressing?

Pray

Consider the process a caterpillar has to go through to transform fully into a butterfly. There is much activity inside, even when the chrysalis appears to be dormant – it takes time. Pray about situations in your life, work or family where change feels like it is a long time coming. Pour out to God any feelings of impatience as you write a prayer on the large chrysalis. Give the process of transformation over to him, accepting that this might take time or happen in unseen ways. You might want to write a prayer for patience and perseverance when change seems slow, or for trusting God to do unseen transformation in your life or the lives of others, believing he can bring renewal and change. Meditate as you look at the chrysalis of prayers on how God can radically redesign us, though we need patience when there appears to be no outward sign of the changes within. Just like the incredible metamorphosis that occurs within the stillness of a dark chrysalis, God makes small changes in us that can be hard to appreciate. Give thanks for those times in the past when God has brought you through a season of waiting, and your prayers and perseverance have seen significant changes in your life and faith development.

Transformation power

Prayer focus

To pray for the confidence to embrace change, appreciating that metamorphosis takes time. To reflect on God's transformation power.

Bible reflection

> [I am] confident of this, that he who began a good work in you will carry it on to completion until the day of Christ Jesus.
> PHILIPPIANS 1:6

What I need

- Tissue paper of various colours, cut into small rectangles
- Wooden clip pegs
- Felt-tip pens
- Small googly eyes
- Pipe cleaners
- PVA glue

Reflect

Caterpillars go through huge stages of change and growth before they are ready to emerge as a butterfly, a new creation. When visible change is not happening in our lives, we can often doubt that God is at work, but he is working to prepare the transformations to come. Do you resist change, feeling secure in the current caterpillar stage of your life and faith? You are called by God to fulfil a purpose. Imagine a caterpillar watching a soaring butterfly, thinking, 'I could never do that,' not realising that within them is the potential to do just that! Are there areas of ministry God has placed on your heart, a new direction you are exploring or a long-held dream or need for healing that just seems unobtainable? When the process of transformation has begun, there may be seasons in which you feel like you have regressed, but God has given you a new life and a new identity. You may not feel like you are a butterfly yet, but you are no longer the caterpillar you once were. Take courage: the old has passed and he is transforming you daily.

Pray

Reflect on the stage you are at in your faith journey, as you create a peg caterpillar. Colour in the peg, stick on tiny googly eyes and pray about the changes you want to see in your life. Be honest with God as you transform the peg into a caterpillar, bringing to him your fears about change and those things that seem utterly impossible. Change takes us out of our comfort zone and requires effort on our part, even leaving the familiar to embrace a new identity. There is much to learn in the caterpillar stages of our faith journey, and we can often be too focused on reaching a goal to appreciate the things God is doing in the time of waiting. When your caterpillar is finished, continue to pray as you clip tissue paper wings into the peg, spreading them out as you reflect on the transformation God has made in your life and praying about ways you want to continue to change. If you do not yet feel ready to add wings and want to pray further about your identity in Christ, take a piece of tissue paper with you, use your peg caterpillar to help you pray for transformation and add the wings at another time.

Butterfly aspirations

Prayer focus

To ask God to help us see the potential butterflies we can be. To trust that he can totally transform our lives and we are no longer the person we once were.

Bible reflection

> Therefore, if anyone is in Christ, he is a new creature; the old things passed away; behold, new things have come.
> 2 CORINTHIANS 5:17 (NASB)

What I need

- A4 construction paper in various colours
- Scissors
- String
- Paint
- Plates or trays (for the paint)
- Wipes/handwashing facilities
- Protective table covering

Fold a sheet of paper in half and cut the outline of one butterfly wing and half the body, so that it opens out to form a symmetrical butterfly shape. Cut lengths of string ready and put trays of paint out.

Reflect

We can take steps to make positive changes in our life, choosing to transform ourselves with a new image, making healthy choices that have an impact on our well-being or making a conscious effort to change the way we behave or think. These can all bring a fresh perspective in our life, but change isn't always easy and to transform we need God's strength. By surrendering ourselves to him, we can become a new creation, chosen and set free. Like a butterfly finally emerging from the chrysalis, we can take flight and live in freedom when we trust God and discover a new identity in Christ. In the Bible, there are many examples of people being renamed when they followed God and were transformed. Just as a butterfly has a new character, no longer called a caterpillar, you have a new beginning as God's beloved, your identity changed and secure in Christ.

Pray

Take a paper butterfly and spend some time considering ways God has already transformed your life, giving you a new identity in Christ. Dip the string into the paint and add it to the right-hand side of the flat paper butterfly, swirling it into any pattern you like on the paper, leaving a small length outside the paper. Fold over the other half of the butterfly and press the top half down gently. While you are doing this, give thanks for the ways God has given you new opportunities in your life and faith journey. Bring to him any changes you want to see in your life, trusting he has incredible, unseen plans for your life as you pull the string from within the folded paper. When you are ready, unfold the butterfly to reveal the beautiful pattern you made, which is unique, just like your personal journey of transformation with God. Enjoy the visual display of vibrant coloured swirls you formed on the butterfly wings and give thanks to God for the unique wings he is preparing for you. Trust that he is preparing you to take flight with confidence. Close by praying for the courage to fly in freedom, in ways only you can, as a new creation.

Reflecting as a church community

9
Family of God

God's family tree

Prayer focus

To reflect on the unique part you play in the family of God. To give thanks to the Lord for the family or community you are part of.

Bible reflection

> Instead, speaking the truth in love, we will grow to become in every respect the mature body of him who is the head, that is, Christ. From him the whole body, joined and held together by every supporting ligament, grows and builds itself up in love, as each part does its work.
>
> EPHESIANS 4:15–16

What I need

- Large sheet of cardboard
- Coloured ink pads
- Pens
- Hand wipes

Draw or print a tree outline on to the cardboard sheet. Put out ink pads and hand wipes ready.

Reflect

We are all part of a family, be it a biological family or a community of like-minded people. Consider your place in your own family, where you may be a child, parent, grandparent, sibling or have several identities. Whatever your relationship with your biological relatives, you are part of God's family. This makes you an important name on a family tree that includes branches spreading worldwide, with brothers and sisters in Christ dating back generations into history that share kinship with you. You are part of God's family tree, a child of God. We each have individual talents, interests and personality traits that set us apart from others. Yet within a family or a community, we often share common interests, inherited leanings towards certain subjects or pastimes and a shared faith.

Pray

Reflect on ways you are like others in your family, perhaps in appearance or values, and ways you are unique. Bring your specific role or place in your family or church to God in prayer, as you reflect on what it means to you to be part of this group of people. Our experience of our biological family may be distant, perhaps even unknown to us, or fraught with relationship issues. Whatever your family circumstances, in following Christ you have been adopted into God's family. You are loved and accepted by your heavenly Father. In response, press your finger into the ink pad and add your fingerprint on to a branch of the family tree. You may want to write your name next to it too. Look at the other prints that have been added, each one completely unique yet part of God's family tree. Pray about the gifts you are blessed with, the things you contribute to the life of your church or wider community or the role you play in your own family. Give thanks to God that you are part of a community, a church or group who represent part of God's worldwide church family. Leave your unique mark, knowing that you have a specific role to play in God's plans and that your contribution is important.

You matter to God

Prayer focus

To reflect on how important you are to God, thanking him for making you unique, with a role only you can fulfil in his plan.

Bible reflection

> Then Jesus told them this parable: 'Suppose one of you has a hundred sheep and loses one of them. Doesn't he leave the ninety-nine in the open country and go after the lost sheep until he finds it? And when he finds it, he joyfully puts it on his shoulders and goes home.'
>
> LUKE 15:3–6

What I need

- Wooden dolly pegs (or wooden spoons)
- Googly eyes
- Material scraps
- Pipe cleaners
- Ribbon
- Wool
- Felt-tip pens
- Glue or sticky tape

Put out a selection of materials for decorating, along with the pegs and felt-tip pens.

Reflect

In any community or group, there are people of different backgrounds, ages, personality types and gifting. We all have our own individual ways of worshipping or using our skills in church, and we all have something unique to bring to the collective experience of praising God together, as a family of believers. What do you do as part of your community to share God's love and support others? Do you realise how precious you are to God? Like the shepherd in the parable of the lost sheep, God would leave the 99 to search for you if you strayed. He delights in you and the unique gifts that you bring to the community you are part of, where each person matters to God.

Pray

Take a plain dolly peg. Hold it as you consider your own unique value: those things you bring to all you do – the part you play in your home, church and community. Spend some time decorating the peg, dressing it, adding a face to represent you. Reflect as you do this. Pray for God to reveal new ways that you can make a difference in the life of your church or community, or give thanks for the opportunities you already have to be an integral part of the community of believers. Know that your contribution is significant, whether you serve coffee, lead worship, make pastoral visits or simply are a regular part of the worshipping congregation, encouraging others in your fellowship. Consider the ways you might step out in faith to share your journey and have opportunities to bless others. Pray through with God any feelings that your talents are less important or useful than those of others. Be assured that we are all important to God. You are made unique for a purpose, and have exactly the gifts you need to fulfil God's plans through you. Ask him to give you a fresh appreciation of how much you matter to him and of your role as part of a community of believers, where everyone has a part to play.

God at the heart of our home

Prayer focus

To place God at the centre of your home and church.

Bible reflection

I pray that out of his glorious riches he may strengthen you with power through his Spirit in your inner being, so that Christ may dwell in your hearts through faith. And I pray that you, being rooted and established in love, may have power, together with all the Lord's holy people, to grasp how wide and long and high and deep is the love of Christ, and to know this love that surpasses knowledge – that you may be filled to the measure of all the fullness of God.

EPHESIANS 3:16–19

What I need

- Cardboard
- Heart-shaped sticky notes
- Scissors
- Pens

Cut out house shapes from the cardboard, big enough to fit a sticky note heart in the centre with space around it. Put these out with the sticky notes and pens.

Reflect

Making God the centre or heart of all we do is important: consciously inviting him to be present and acknowledging him as part of our church, home and wherever we are. We so often forget to seek him first, to look to him as a focal point in our decision-making and to direct our words, actions and thoughts. In following God, we need habitually to make him our first point of reference as we navigate daily life. We can get so caught up in practicalities or in trying to sort things ourselves that, even in ministry or church life, we forget to seek God's direction. Instead, we need to place him at the centre of all we are doing, living and working for his glory. Do you bring your daily life and concerns to God, or has he become less of a priority?

Pray

Meditate on the place God occupies in your life. Do you put him at the centre of all you do, in your home, church, workplace or community? Or has he been sidelined, as your reliance on God as the central source of your faith and strength has dwindled? Spending time with God may have gradually become less frequent, as you balance responsibilities and have invested time and energy into other relationships. Take a cardboard house. Then take a sticky note heart and write on it – perhaps simply 'God' or a prayer – as you ask God to forgive you and resolve to make him central in your life again – the very heart of all you do. Stick the heart firmly in the centre of your house, praying that God might be found at the centre of yourself and that he might make a home in your heart. If you need to, use this response to ask God into your heart as Saviour again, to fill your inner being afresh with him and to make him the central focus around which you build your other relationships and all aspects of your daily life.

Every piece of a jigsaw is needed

Prayer focus

To know that your part in God's plan is important, just as every piece of a jigsaw is needed for the picture to be complete.

Bible reflection

> For just as each of us has one body with many members, and these members do not all have the same function, so in Christ we, though many, form one body, and each member belongs to all the others. We have different gifts, according to the grace given to each of us.
> ROMANS 12:4–6

What I need

- Card
- Scissors
- Marker pen or printer
- Jigsaw puzzle (with suitable number of pieces for your group)
- Board or table to set the jigsaw out on
- Pens

Cut out jigsaw-piece-shaped cards, with the words 'Every piece is needed' and 'Romans 12:4–6' written or printed on them. Set out the jigsaw puzzle. You may want to have sections of the jigsaw already done, with gaps left to fill in during the prayer response.

Reflect

The pieces of a jigsaw puzzle, when seen individually, can be difficult to identify clearly. This is particularly true in a puzzle with a large number of pieces, where a tiny blue piece could be part of the sky or just as easily form a small section of a vast sea. Yet each unique piece can only fit in a certain place and has a specific role in the whole picture. If even a single piece is missing from a jigsaw, the image remains incomplete; even the most insignificant-looking piece is needed. A jigsaw piece by itself serves no function; it can be unclear what it depicts when it is seen separate from the whole picture. It needs to be connected to the other pieces that surround it, working in unison to fulfil its purpose and complete the image on the jigsaw.

Pray

Reflect on the important part each of us has to play as a member of our family, church and community. Respond by writing your name or a short prayer on the blank reverse of a jigsaw piece and adding this to the bigger picture, as you pray about the role you play in the bigger picture of your work or your church ministry. Bring to God any feelings of unworthiness or doubt about the contribution you can make. Know that you matter to God and believe that the things you do are significant, as you add your piece to the full picture, where every piece needs to be present. Your jigsaw piece is connected to others around it, securing it and bringing strength, as part of the whole jigsaw. Leave your piece firmly in its unique, appointed place as a confirmation of your prayers and a symbol of wanting to play your part in God's plan. Take with you a jigsaw-piece-shaped card, to remind you that every piece is needed. You are important to God and he created you the exact shape you needed to be to fit in the picture that is his plan.

10
Love is...
Reflections on 1 Corinthians 13

Love is… patient

Prayer focus

To pray for patience towards others and the strength to forgive and let go of hurts and grievances.

Bible reflection

> Bear with each other and forgive one another if any of you has a grievance against someone. Forgive as the Lord forgave you.
> COLOSSIANS 3:13

What I need

- Red and yellow card
- Scissors
- Marker pens/felt-tip pens
- Glue stick
- Laminator and laminating pouches (optional)

Cut out red and yellow circles of equal size from the card. Draw angry faces on the red ones and happy faces on the yellow ones. Glue one of each face back to back. Laminate them if you wish. Lay the faces out with the red side up, concealing the happy face underneath.

Reflect

Patience is a fruit of the Holy Spirit, but it can be one of the most difficult attitudes to have when other people cause us to feel a grievance towards them. Patience is not easy to show but is a loving response. The reference to love being 'patient', in 1 Corinthians 13, is from the Greek word meaning 'long-tempered'. Who are the people in your life who test your patience or are the most difficult to show this kind of love to? People we love most dearly can provoke the strongest emotions in us, causing us to lose our patience with them easily, and some people seem to deliberately incite confrontations. God calls us to let go of grievances, to forgive those who hurt us and to not hold on to anger. How could you show this kind of love to others, choosing a 'long-tempered' attitude in situations where you would normally react impatiently?

Pray

Look at the angry faces before you and think about specific times when you responded with impatience or anger. Have you been upset or hurt by someone in the past and not fully forgiven the person, still remembering the grievance today? Use this prayer response to face these past hurts and bring them before God, asking him to help you forgive. Reflect on situations where you were impatient, and think of ways you could have reacted differently, asking God to give you the grace and strength to show patience towards others in your daily life.

Turn over an angry face as your response and as a symbol of your seeking God's strength to show patience, revealing a smiling face as you let go of hurts and grievances in prayer. Take the face away with you, as a reminder to continue to pray for patience, turn from anger and forgive those who upset you. It can take time and prayer to move on from hurts that deeply affect us. Seek out someone to talk to and pray with you if you feel you need further support with the things this prayer has brought up for you.

Love is… kind

Prayer focus

To think of others you might find hard to love, making a gift for them and praying for them. To share the gift of God's love with others.

Bible reflection

> Gracious words are a honeycomb, sweet to the soul and healing to the bones.
> PROVERBS 16:24

What I need

- Printer or pens
- Cardboard
- Scissors
- Selection of little gifts (e.g. wrapped chocolates or sweets)
- Bowls
- Organza bags

Produce small verse cards with the words of 1 Corinthians 13:4–7 or Proverbs 16:24 printed or written on them. Fill bowls with a variety of treats and put out the organza bags.

Reflect

Being kind can sound like a gentle, soft expression of feeling towards someone, yet to be kind to those who aren't always kind to us takes real strength of character. Kindness is an outward sign of love and a practical expression of God's love. The NIV translation of Proverbs 16:24 uses the word 'gracious' in place of 'kind'. Being kind to others isn't always easy, but it is a way of showing grace, God's grace. In some versions of the Bible, the word 'love' in 1 Corinthians 13 is replaced with the word 'charity'. In this context, charity means a giving and benevolent attitude towards others that comes from our devotion to God and his love for us. The Greek word is *agape*, which is the highest form of love; it is selfless and transcends circumstances. Charity in this sense is the translation of God's love for us, expressed as we direct it to others.

Pray

Take an organza bag and select some treats from the bowls, praying as you prepare this small gift for the person you intend to give it to. This may be someone you find it difficult to show love and kindness towards, or you could give it to someone as an expression of God's love for them. What other acts of charity and *agape* love could you do to show love graciously to others? Giving this bag away rather than keeping it for yourself is a symbol of your desire to be charitable, showing kindness to others. Add a verse card to the bag. Challenge yourself to find ways to show kindness in your words and deeds, particularly towards those people who you find difficult to love, and extend grace to them. Ask God as you pray and reflect on this to give you opportunities to share his *agape* love and demonstrate kindness and grace. Pray that as you give this gift away it might bless the recipient, reflecting God's love as you make a conscious effort to show kindness in your words and deeds. Take a verse card home for yourself, as a reminder to show charity towards others and to remember the incredible, selfless love God has for you.

Love... keeps no record of wrong

Prayer focus

To let go of grievances. To ask for God's help to forgive those who have wronged you.

Bible reflection

> You must put away all bitterness, anger, wrath, quarrelling, and slanderous talk – indeed all malice. Instead, be kind to one another, compassionate, forgiving one another, just as God in Christ also forgave you.
> EPHESIANS 4:31–32 (NET)

What I need

- A4 white paper or card
- Pencils
- Red poster paint
- Pots/jars for water
- Paintbrushes
- Protective table covering

Reflect

Long after someone has wronged us, we often hold a record of it deep inside. This can cause us to carry around resentment and bitterness for days, weeks, months or even years afterwards. Are there long-held hurts that you struggle to forgive as the remembrance of them still causes you pain, though you want to react in Christian love? You may not even realise how deeply someone has offended you and how much effect a slight has had on you. God does not keep a record of our transgressions; when we ask for forgiveness and truly repent, the slate is wiped clean. To love others with the same love that God has shown us, we need to find ways to let go of hurts caused by others in order to live in freedom. It is virtually impossible to forget the negative experiences we have encountered, but we can choose to seek God's strength and healing to take steps to forgive those who have wronged us.

Pray

Take a sheet of paper and pencil. Begin to pray about the people and situations you have reflected on, past or present. Write your own 'record of wrongs'. This might be a list of people who have hurt you or the circumstances that upset you. Bring any feelings of bitterness or unresolved anger to God in prayer. When you are ready, take a paintbrush and cover these transgressions with a good layer of red paint. Ask God to help you let go of the feelings you have harboured and to seek guidance if any of the situations are currently affecting your peace. Pray for a fresh experience of his grace and the strength to overcome any residual feelings.

You may need to seek prayer support about some of the feelings this prayer has been addressing for you. As you close your time of prayer, take some time to look at the page, now awash with red and with the wrongs almost entirely eradicated by the paint. Reflect on this as a symbol of the blood of Jesus that washes away sin and means we can be forgiven for our transgressions. Ask God for the strength to live in the freedom that Christ bought for you upon the cross, as you seek to live a life of forgiveness and to let go of any hurts.

Love… does not envy

Prayer focus

To soften our jealous heart and replace it with a heart of love. To ask God to forgive our pride or envy.

Bible reflection

'I will give you a new heart and put a new spirit in you; I will remove from you your heart of stone and give you a heart of flesh.'
EZEKIEL 36:26

What I need

- Green modelling dough
- Small pebbles
- Plastic boards or plates
- Protective table covering

Roll the modelling dough into small balls with a pebble at the centre, covered completely so it isn't visible. Put out boards or plastic plates.

Reflect

Jealousy is not an emotion we like to admit to. When we envy someone else's achievements, home, job or position in ministry, this can poison our hearts. It makes our hearts hard and sets up feelings of dissatisfaction towards our own life or abilities. We may not even realise how deeply this resentment of others can steal our joy, when we draw comparison with our own lives. Love calls us not to focus on our personal desires or selfish jealousy, which can lead to anger and dissatisfaction and which are in direct conflict with the selfless love God shows us. Paul chastises the Corinthian church, as he writes about the gifts of the Spirit, for comparing their spiritual gifts and setting some of their congregation above others in importance. Yet Paul is clear that, as Christians, we should be building each other up and encouraging fellow believers in the use of their gifts, not being envious of the gifts given to them.

Pray

Take a lump of modelling dough in your hands. Begin to soften it as you reflect on the verse from Ezekiel. Consider the ways God has changed you, inside and out, on your journey of faith, softening your heart. Enjoy the relaxing tactile experience of softening the dough, while you bring your reflections to God. Find within the centre of the modelling dough a 'heart of stone'. Remove this as you respond to the verse, asking God to remove from you any hard feelings you hold towards others, feelings of envy or jealousy that have hardened your heart. Put the stone to one side and focus on moulding the dough into a softened ball, then into the shape of a heart. Give thanks to God for the ways he has reshaped your heart and ask him to help you reject feelings of jealousy, to instead focus on all the gifts and blessings he has filled your life with.

When you are ready to close your time of prayer, leave the stone behind and take with you the heart you created, as a reminder of the new heart God has given you. Use it as a prompt to reject feelings of jealousy and to give thanks for your gifts.

11
Armour of God

Belt of truth

Prayer focus

The truth of God can protect us from the enemy's lies that we might be tempted to believe about ourselves.

Bible reflection

> But the Lord is with me like a mighty warrior; so my persecutors will stumble and not prevail. They will fail and be thoroughly disgraced; their dishonour will never be forgotten.
>
> JEREMIAH 20:11

What I need

- Sheets of scraperboard
- Scissors
- Scraper art tools
- Sticky tape (optional)

Cut our strips of scraperboard. Lay these out along with the inscribing tools.

Reflect

We can get caught up in the untruths that others hold about us or the paralysing lies that the enemy whispers to us in our weak moments, using our own insecurities to create in our heart and mind a false view of our worth or ability. Doubts can creep slowly into our thinking, yet we need to focus firmly on the truth of God's promises and his view of us, trusting him to encircle us with a belt of truth to protect us from Satan's lies. Consider ways you are influenced by the opinions of others or your own thinking about yourself that is contradictory to the truth of God's love and that gives the enemy room to plant seeds of doubt in your mind, which, over time, may take root. God's love shines out of even the darkest situations when we choose to claim the truth of his grace and power as protection against the lies of the enemy, which seek to infiltrate our thinking.

Pray

Take some time to think of those things that stop you being able to focus on God's truth, as you look at the black scraperboard. Write words or prayers using the tools provided, declaring God's truth over lies that attack our peace. The words you write will allow the colour, light and clarity to shine through, as you press firmly into the dark scraperboard. Brush away the specks of dark material that form as you inscribe your words of truth. As you finish your time of prayer, reflect on ways you can surround yourself with God's messages of love and with a knowledge of his strength to defend you. The truth of God's word can protect us, surrounding us with the armour and strength of God to stand firm against the enemy's falsehood, the words of others and even the lies we tell ourselves about our worth. Your prayer 'belt of truth' can then be taped together with those written by others to create a large collective belt of truth – or you can take up your individual belt, wear it around your wrist or place it somewhere you will see it, as a reminder of God's protection encircling you.

Shield of faith

Prayer focus

God is our defender and shield in times of trouble. To thank God for the ways he protects and shields us. To ask for his protection.

Bible reflection

'As for God, his way is perfect: the Lord's word is flawless; he shields all who take refuge in him.'
2 SAMUEL 22:31

What I need

- Large sheet of cardboard
- Pens or pencils
- Scissors

Draw a large shield outline on the cardboard, with a wide cross in the middle, dividing it into four, with the four parts of the cross extending to the edge. You may want to cut out the shield shape. Put out pens or pencils ready.

Reflect

There are many circumstances that come against us in our daily faith journey and in our everyday life that might strike a blow to our confidence. There are subtle ways that the enemy can attempt to stop us in our tracks or wound our faith, as we seek to stand for God's love and face spiritual battles head-on. Take some time to reflect on any ways you feel under attack or in need of refuge. Look at the shield before you, with the cross at the centre representing Christ's victory over death and sin, which gives us freedom from Satan's schemes. Know that the fiery arrows of the enemy are no match for the shield of God's promises, the protection we can know when we trust that he is fighting for us and giving us the strength to persevere.

Pray

Think about setbacks, events or temptations that come between you and all the things you would like to do for God. Perhaps you feel vulnerable or under attack from the devil or by the words or deeds of others. Remember that victory is ours through Christ Jesus and that God is your shield and refuge. Give thanks to God that our hope is in him and that through Jesus' sacrifice on the cross we are protected. Write a prayer or words of thanks on the shield, bringing to God those areas of your life where you feel you need a greater sense of his protection, asking for the strength to take up the shield of his word against the devil's attacks.

Helmet of salvation

Prayer focus

To reflect on the power of God's salvation truth, which can protect us, like a helmet, from external worries and internal thinking that overwhelms our mind.

Bible reflection

> And the peace of God, which transcends all understanding, will guard your hearts and your minds in Christ Jesus.
> PHILIPPIANS 4:7

What I need

- Newspaper
- Flour
- Water
- Bowls
- Balloons
- Protective table covering
- Empty yoghurt pots or similar
- Metallic paint (optional)
- Paintbrushes (optional)

Tear the newspaper into small strips/pieces. Mix a paste of flour and water in some bowls. Make sure the paste is a gloopy consistency to coat the strips of paper, neither too thick nor watery. Put these out ready along with the balloons and the paint/paintbrushes, if using.

Reflect

Our minds can often become filled with so many things. The demands of daily life can cloud our minds and leave us feeling overwhelmed. Our thoughts can race with anxiety as we try to process so many different issues and we can be left feeling bombarded and unable to cope with the demands placed on us. Internal stresses can also build up, leaving us feeling like we are failing to manage on lots of levels. The enemy will use our vulnerable times, whispering doubt into our already exhausted mind. Do you have things that fill your mind and cause you to feel inundated with concerns? God wants us to put on a helmet of salvation, to ask him to protect our minds with the solid truth of his love and strength.

Pray

Blow up a balloon. Watch your breath filling the balloon and think of all that is currently filling your mind: things you are worried about, responsibilities you have or concerns for others. Perhaps you are also filling your mind with negative influences from the people around you, world issues or absorbing the concerns of others. When you have tied the balloon, balance it on a yoghurt pot. Dip strips of newspaper in the glue mixture and add them on to your balloon (leaving a gap at the bottom so that it will fit on to your head when dry). Pray as you layer them across the round surface and across each other. Bring to God those things that crowd your mind. Reflect on the softness of the paper mâché, yet notice how strong a material it becomes, making a firm layer around the balloon when it dries. God knows our vulnerabilities and every worried thought that fills our mind, and he wants us to clothe ourselves with his strength, in our weakness. Pray, as you create a helmet, for God's strength to surround your mind, to guard your thoughts and to replace your worries with a knowledge of his power and gentle love surrounding us at all times, that we might choose to give into his care the thoughts and concerns that can invade our minds.

Optionally, paint the helmet when it has dried, then pop the balloon. You might want to use your helmet as part of a display or as a prop for Bible storytelling.

Sword of the Spirit

Prayer focus

God's word can be our weapon against lies and attack when we face spiritual battles. To pray for God's love to guard us against the things that come against us, as we stand for him.

Bible reflection

> For the word of God is alive and active. Sharper than any double-edged sword, it penetrates even to dividing soul and spirit, joints and marrow; it judges the thoughts and attitudes of the heart.
>
> HEBREWS 4:12

What I need

- Thick cardboard (cardboard box or similar)
- Marker pen
- Scissors
- Tinfoil
- Sticky tape
- Pencils (not sharpened) or blunt scraperboard tool

Cut out the shape of a large, old-fashioned sword from the cardboard. Cover the blade with a smooth sheet of shiny tinfoil, securing it on the back with sticky tape, making a taut surface to write on. Put this and the writing tools out ready.

Reflect

We often think of a sword as a weapon to wound an assailant in battle, yet it is also used to protect the bearer from the enemy when they attack. A skilled swordsman can use his weapon to deflect the many jabs and swipes of an opponent's sword. God's Spirit and the truth of his word are described in scripture as being like a sword, a strong weapon in our hands that can protect us against the many onslaughts of the devil. In preparing ourselves for spiritual battles, we can arm ourselves with the truth of God's word and the strength of his Holy Spirit to defend against the enemy's advances.

Pray

Reflect on anything you are facing at the moment that feels like a battle. This might be a situation at work, at home or even in church where you are dealing with opposition or attack from others, in word or deed. Know that in all circumstances God is with us and wants us to stand firm. We possess the truth of his word and promises, so no enemy can triumph against us. There may be spiritual elements to the onslaughts you are experiencing, and you might need to ask God for the strength to speak out with the weapon of the sword of the Spirit – God's word that is more powerful than any weapon forged against us. When you have meditated on these things, write prayers or words on the blade with the tools provided, as a symbol of your taking up the sword of the Spirit. Believe that you can be defended by God's words of truth in scripture and claim these afresh as you face spiritual battles and conflicts, asking for God's word to be your protection.

12
Firm foundation in God

Building on the rock

Prayer focus

To build our lives on a firm foundation of trust in God and his word.

Bible reflection

'Everyone then who hears these words of mine and does them will be like a wise man who built his house on the rock. And the rain fell, and the floods came, and the winds blew and beat on that house, but it did not fall, because it had been founded on the rock.'

MATTHEW 7:24–25 (ESV)

What I need

- Coloured toy building bricks
- Marker pen or fine-line marker
- Base board (optional)
- Bowl/tray

Put out the toy bricks (on the base board, if using), perhaps connecting a few together as part of a wall. Write on some other loose bricks the words 'God is our firm foundation' and 'Matthew 7:24–25'. Put these bricks out separately, in a bowl or tray.

Reflect

We can sometimes rely on the wrong things in life, putting our faith in relationships which ultimately let us down or building a foundation on our career or the possessions we own. These can be temporary and can suddenly change, like shifting sand beneath us. If we were building a house, we would not choose to construct it without firm and deep foundations, yet we build our lives on things that cannot withstand storms or sustain us. What do you build your trust upon in your life? Do you find security in the promises of others or the material things you have? Jesus' parable of the wise and foolish builders speaks of the foundation we should build our lives upon, the solid rock that is God. Do you need to dig deeper foundations with God, to help you withstand the storms of life, not putting your faith in relationships, situations or material things that are temporal and temporary?

Pray

Take some bricks and begin to construct the walls of a building, upon the firm base if provided. While you use the toy bricks to make a solid structure, grounded firmly on rigid foundations, reflect upon the ways God has provided you with a safe grounding to withstand the fierce winds and rain of life. Prayerfully give thanks to God for his strength and faithfulness, his guiding hand that keeps you steady. Bring to God any areas of your life that feel less certain: perhaps changes you are facing or relationships or health issues that feel rather like shifting sand beneath you. Acknowledge any ways you have built your life on things other than God, as you fix together the bricks. Take time to ask God to help you know where to place your confidence and to resist the temptation to place your trust in anything else. Commit again, as you secure the bricks, to building your life on the rock that is God, your firm foundation. Take away with you a brick with the words 'God is our firm foundation' on it as a reminder to place your trust in the security of God's hands and to build your life on the firm foundation of the rock.

Jesus, our cornerstone

Prayer focus

To reflect on Jesus as the cornerstone of our faith, the crucial stone that the Christian church is built upon. To put Christ first and work in unity as a body of believers.

Bible reflection

[You are] built on the foundation of the apostles and prophets, with Christ Jesus himself as the chief cornerstone.
EPHESIANS 2:20

What I need

- Buttercream (recipe available online or in baking books)
- Bowls
- Spoons
- Brick-shaped biscuits (e.g. shortbread fingers or custard creams)
- Disposable plates
- Protective table covering
- Hand wipes or handwashing facilities

Prepare plenty of buttercream in advance and put this out in bowls with spoons and the biscuits. Place out disposable plates.

Reflect

The cornerstone is a crucial part of a structure, giving strength and support to the rest of the surrounding bricks and the building as a whole. Jesus is referred to in scripture as the chief foundation stone on which the New Testament church is built: the chief cornerstone, the strongest and most solid stone. Jesus also describes himself as the cornerstone upon which the whole church will be built as a unified body. In order to build and grow our church, we need to set Jesus at the base of everything we do, the strength on which we build our faith community. How can we be united as a body of believers, committing to building the church upon the foundation Jesus laid?

Pray

Build a wall of biscuits, using them as bricks and cementing them together with the buttercream. While you are doing this, reflect on what it means to you as an individual and as part of your church community to place Jesus as the foundation of your faith, and to set him as the cornerstone of all you do and the one who deserves praise and worship. Consider times you may have neglected to build upon Jesus as the founder of the church and ways you need to come back to him as the source of your strength rather than trying to build on insecure foundations. You might want to connect your wall with those made by others as a symbol of seeking to be a united body of believers, building your church on the solid teachings of Jesus. Enjoy eating your biscuit wall as you reflect on the cornerstone of your faith, giving thanks for his steadfast love.

Stronger together

Prayer focus

To reflect on church being stronger together, each playing our unique part. To use our gifts to build each other up, standing firm together with God as our guide.

Bible reflection

> So Christ himself gave the apostles, the prophets, the evangelists, the pastors and teachers, to equip his people for works of service, so that the body of Christ may be built up until we all reach unity in the faith and in the knowledge of the Son of God and become mature, attaining to the whole measure of the fullness of Christ.
>
> EPHESIANS 4:11–13

What I need

- Rectangular wooden blocks (e.g. from a wooden tower game)
- Table

Reflect

Community develops from an instinct to gather with like-minded people. A church is at heart a community, with people choosing to join it from many different backgrounds. In a church, people of all ages, races and life experiences share a desire to worship God and meet with others to pray, learn and grow in faith. In any group, it is inevitable that there will be differences of opinions and even strong division, with many different personalities trying to coexist. Are there times you find it difficult being part of your church community? What are the benefits to being part of a collective of Christians within your wider community? There is great strength in diversity, when it is used to positive effect. Finding ways to work together as a church, building each other up and recognising our differences and individual strengths brings unity in the structure of our church community.

Pray

Take a wooden block. Hold it as you reflect on your unique gifts and the contributions you make to your church community. Pray to let go of any feelings of inadequacy and know that God has a role for you that only you can fulfil. When you are ready, place your block alongside others in a row of three, with each new layer of three being placed horizontally perpendicular to the last, thus making a strong tower. If you're doing this as a congregational response, place the single block that represents you. If doing it as a station, you may want to add a few more blocks to represent those who support you, praying for them. Give thanks that each of us have our own particular strengths we can contribute to the whole. The blocks do not have much use on their own, but they are each important when they become part of the strong tower of faith you have created. Pray for a fresh discerning of your own gifts from God and how you can use these as part of a body of believers. The blocks in the tower have to be placed carefully so that they don't fall. Reflect upon the ways we need to be gentle with each other, appreciating each person's differing perspectives, yet also standing side by side in prayer and friendship to create a solid place from which to glorify God together.

Building the church

Prayer focus

To reflect on the ways we are playing our part in building God's church in our community, on a firm foundation of faith. To thank God for his provision. To seek a vision for how to see further growth.

Bible reflection

'And I tell you that you are Peter, and on this rock I will build my church, and the gates of Hades will not overcome it.'
MATTHEW 16:18

What I need

- Rectangular ice cream wafers
- Ice cream cones
- Selection of biscuits
- Various sweets to decorate
- Writing icing
- Desiccated coconut
- Green food colouring
- Jelly people sweets
- Buttercream
- Bowls
- Trays or paper plates

Make buttercream and put out wafers, cones, sweets and icing. Mix green food colouring into the desiccated coconut.

Reflect

A traditional church building is instantly recognisable, with its historical features like a steeple or bell tower and stained-glass windows. However, many church congregations meet in other types of buildings that are not so obviously a church. Community centres, homes, schools and even theatres and cinemas are used for those wanting to meet to praise God and regularly share fellowship and teaching. The physical building in which a congregation gathers matters far less than the commitment and unity of those joining together as people of God. It is the people, not the bricks and mortar, who are building God's church in our community. A traditional church building may give a strong visible presence in the heart of a community, but it is the resources and outreach provided by the people who populate the church that matter, as well as the impact our faith has inside and outside the walls where we meet.

Pray

Reflect on the strengths of your church community, whether you meet in a lofty church with pews, a community venue or someone's home. Have fun building an edible church, icing together the wafers to create walls, a roof and an ice cream cone steeple! Decorate the structure, adding icing windows and doors, green dessicated coconut as grass outside and even jelly people sweets for the congregation. Pray about the ways your faith community is 'building' God's church within your local area, giving thanks for the physical building he has provided and the people who are the church. Ask God to inspire you to see outside the walls of your church building, to find new ways to reach out to the wider community, challenging stereotypical views of traditional church, building on the foundations of your faith. Give thanks to God for the space and resources you have as you finish building your edible church. Break down the walls and enjoy eating the church, whilst considering ways you can break down the metaphorical walls to reach out to those in your community, by inviting them to church or taking the message of God's love out into the surrounding area in new ways.

Reflecting on our faith journey

13
Shining the light of God

Cross of light

Prayer focus

To pray for God's light to shine in dark places. To stand together in fellowship, that we might be a light in our community, home or workplace.

Bible reflection

But if we walk in the light, as he is in the light, we have fellowship with one another, and the blood of Jesus, his Son, purifies us from all sin.
1 JOHN 1:7

What I need

- Cardboard or metal sheet
- Scissors or metal-cutting tool
- Tea lights (real or electric)
- Suitable floor to lay tea lights out
- Matches or lighter (if using real tea lights)

Cut out a large cross shape from the metal or cardboard sheet. Place tea lights out ready along with matches or lighters if needed.

Reflect

Jesus was sent as a light to shine in dark places and bring God's message of hope and salvation to the world. He didn't carry this news alone; he travelled with trusted companions and met with others in fellowship as he journeyed from place to place, teaching and healing. The Saviour of the world looked to others for prayer and support in his mission and left with them the great commission, to be a light in the darkness and to share with the world the good news of God's love. Just like Jesus, we need to seek encouragement from others and unite with those who also want to shine for God. The empty cross before you reflects a powerful image of Jesus' power over death, and he invites us to add our light to the many people who stood firm, going back in history, and those who stand now across the globe, in the common cause of sharing God's love and shining his light in the world.

Pray

Select an unlit tea light and hold it as you begin to pray. Consider those ways you as an individual can more actively shine God's light in your community. You may want to pray for specific people or groups known to you who do not yet know the light and love of God and the hope that is ours through Jesus' sacrifice on the cross. Light your candle and place it on the cross outline. It is part of a cross of lights, representing the people you walk with in your faith. As you add your individual light to a collective of candles, reflect on how you can support and encourage others to shine their light or ways you need to ask others to stand with you in fellowship and prayer. Make this your commitment to working together to shine God's light in your community as you represent Jesus in our world.

Take another tea light home with you. Light it as a reminder to pray for opportunities to shine like a flame in the world and to reflect the light and love of God in your words and actions. Take time to seek fellow Christians to pray and encourage each other in your mission to be a beacon of light in your community.

Hope shining in the darkness

Prayer focus

Jesus is the light of life and brings hope in dark times. The world can seem dark, but when we follow Jesus we have the light of life, amid even the hardest times.

Bible reflection

> When Jesus spoke again to the people, he said, 'I am the light of the world. Whoever follows me will never walk in darkness, but will have the light of life.'
> JOHN 8:12

What I need

- Yellow cardboard
- Printer or pens
- Chalkboard on stand or easel
- Yellow sticky notes
- Paper
- Scissors

Produce bright yellow verse cards with Jesus' words from John 8 printed or written on them. Set the chalkboard up on the stand or easel, and put plenty of yellow sticky notes and the verse cards out ready.

Reflect

There are times when the world seems to be a very dark place. Stories in the media paint a bleak picture and the news is dominated by scenes of a broken, hurting world. In our own lives, or those of the people close to us, life can be a struggle and darkness can cloud in, overwhelming us. Hope might be a dim flicker, almost snuffed out by our circumstances. God sent Jesus to bring light and hope, a hope that can never be extinguished by darkness. He walks with us and we are called to carry his 'light of life' into the world.

Pray

Look at the black surface of the chalkboard, so dark no light could permeate it. Yet, as you pray, add your yellow sticky note to the board, asking God to bring light into the dark and difficult situations known to you or being experienced in the world today. Even with just one small sticky note added, the darkness is pierced with light, a symbol of Jesus' victory over death and sin. Pray that you might find ways to be a light in the world, sharing the hope of Jesus with others, and trust that God can bring light where there was none.

Reflect on the unstoppable power of light over darkness as others add their sticky notes. The patches of yellow, when placed together, will become so much larger than the black of the chalkboard, now barely visible as light overcomes darkness, covering it with hope.

Take a verse card away with you as a reminder to trust in the light of hope that Jesus brings, even in dark times.

Light under a bowl

Prayer focus

To pray for the courage to shine our light, use our gifts and step out of our comfort zone. To seek God's strength to shine boldly with the love and light of Christ.

Bible reflection

> 'No one lights a lamp and puts it in a place where it will be hidden, or under a bowl. Instead they put it on its stand, so that those who come in may see the light.'
> LUKE 11:33

What I need

- Tea lights (real or electric)
- Large heatproof bowls
- Matches or lighter (if using real tea lights)

Reflect

It can take courage to share our talents and confidence to shine in our own unique way, at home, in our church or in our workplace. Do you feel reluctant to share about a skill or gifting you have, yet you would like to be confident in using it to God's glory? Are you too shy or nervous to step out, wondering how others might react? Do you have a talent for singing, playing an instrument, relating well to children or offering hospitality? Has God been prompting you to speak to someone and share your faith or perhaps you sense a calling on your life to voluntary or ordained ministry? It takes bravery to try something new, to offer to share publicly the talents God has nurtured in you. This verse reminds us not to hide away but to use our God-given abilities, not concealing them so that they cannot reflect God's light. When you bring your reticence and fears to God in prayer, he can help you to take steps to fulfilling your unique purpose and potential.

Pray

Begin by thinking about opportunities you are perhaps nervous to pursue or by asking God to show you ways to share your gifts and let your faith shine brightly. While you light a tea light, ask him to reveal ways you can radiate his love, however much you might feel you lack the skills to shine. Place the light under a bowl, watching as its glow diminishes then vanishes when it is covered (or, if you are using an electric tea light, watch how the light is gradually hidden from sight). Be honest with God about ways you are hiding your light or times the words or actions of others have made you retreat. Bring to him the worries and reluctance that hold you back. You may need to ask God to remove obstacles that stop you shining for him and for the courage to speak out about your faith. When you are ready, remove the bowl, light the tea light again (if required) and allow the light to shine forth, unobscured. Close by praying that God would help you to shine for him. Take another tea light away with you as a reminder to seek God's guidance in discerning opportunities to let your light shine and the courage to set the light of your faith on a stand, for all to see.

Keep my lamp burning

Prayer focus

God keeps our lamp burning, helping us to keep going in our faith and to share the gift of light with others.

Bible reflection

> You, Lord, keep my lamp burning; my God turns my darkness into light.
> PSALM 18:28

What I need

- Clear glass candle holders or smooth, clear glass tumblers
- Glass pens or paint
- Paintbrushes (if using paint)
- Tea lights
- Protective table covering

Reflect

It can be hard to share God's light and love with others when we ourselves feel disheartened or tired or are dealing with our own troubles. Psalm 18 reflects with thanksgiving that God sustains us. He is the oil that keeps our lamps of faith burning even in dark times, the fuel that keeps us shining. God can give us the strength to keep sharing his light and love in the world, turning our darkness into light. Are there ways you feel the light of your faith or your enthusiasm for telling of God's great love has dimmed? Do you need to ask God for a fresh supply of the fuel of his Holy Spirit to inspire you to radiate his light in your life?

Pray

Spend some time reflecting on the verse from Psalm 18, as you use the pens or paints to decorate a glass candle holder. Bring your prayers to God for his strength to shine before others as you add brightly coloured patterns or a drawing to the glass. You might want to write words about light, a Bible verse or a prayer, as you consider ways you can shine once more for God, or give thanks for the ways he has already helped you tell others about his love and light, which can overcome darkness. When you have finished decorating the glass, put a candle in the holder. Respond to God by lighting the candle, as you acknowledge him as your source of the fuel that keeps your faith burning. Watch as the light from the candle illuminates the colours and words you added and think of ways you can share God's light with others. Take your candle holder home and use it to reflect on ways you can continue to shine for God. Or you may choose to give it to someone as a gift, as you explain to them the way God's love and light have made a difference in your life and pass this light on.

14
God with us on the journey

When the path ahead is unclear

Prayer focus

To trust God when the path before us isn't clear, praying that God would guide us, give us courage and lead us on the right path in our life.

Bible reflection

Trust in the Lord with all your heart and lean not on your own understanding; in all your ways submit to him, and he will make your paths straight.

PROVERBS 3:5–6

What I need

- Large sheet of plain paper or cardboard, or A4 plain paper
- Pens or pencil crayons
- Large sheet and masking tape (optional)

Put out either a large sheet of paper for all to doodle on or an individual A4 sheet of paper per person. You may want to secure a large sheet to the table or other flat surface with masking tape.

Reflect

When we walk along an unfamiliar path, not knowing where it leads, we have no idea what awaits us. What might the terrain be like? If the sun is in our eyes or the pathway turns a corner, we may be unable to see ahead. We have to choose whether to journey onwards, though the way ahead is unknown. In our walk of faith, God is with us on the journey and knows each twist and turn we will encounter and every difficult situation life will present us. When we walk with God, the road may not be as we expected, but he calls us to trust that he journeys with us and knows the path ahead. It may be unclear to us and we may end up in surprising places, walking paths that are muddy, unmarked or precarious, but God walks beside us and has ordained the road ahead.

Pray

Take a pen and begin at a point on the page, drawing a path. This doodle response can be as simple or creative as you like. Reflect on the journey you are taking with God and the obstacles you might be facing. You might want to doodle a winding path, one that goes over rivers, hits a dead end then reroutes or perhaps goes through calming scenery or muddy terrain. While you are drawing, spend time praying that God will help you understand when the path isn't the one you expected or seems so unclear. Your doodled path might meet a crossroads or intersect with the paths of others (if you are doing the activity collectively on a large sheet). Use this as part of your prayer meditation knowing that, whatever path your life takes, God goes with you. Trust in him as your guide when the way ahead is unknown or hidden, or when your path has changed or broken.

Not the way you would have chosen

Prayer focus

To pray for the strength to believe that God will carry us through the hardest of times, when we can no longer walk or even pray for ourselves. When we can't put one foot in front of the other, God carries us.

Bible reflection

'Even to your old age and grey hairs I am he, I am he who will sustain you. I have made you and I will carry you; I will sustain you and I will rescue you.'
ISAIAH 46:4

What I need

- Large marbles
- A4 plain paper
- Plastic trays
- Paint
- Bowls
- Wipes/handwashing facilities
- Protective table covering

Put paint into the bowls. Place out the trays for the paper and marbles.

Reflect

The path our life takes may not be the journey we would have chosen and we may need to walk the same path many times in life. This is not failure, though it feels like going over old ground. God may deliberately lead us on familiar paths to show us how much we have moved forward. We might go through the same journey of illness, relationship issues or hurts many times, but God is with us and uses these paths to help us grow and change. When we tread again painful pathways we had hoped to avoid, we can ultimately find fresh purpose. Retracing our steps along familiar paths can still reveal new things to us, such as fresh experiences of God's grace or opportunities to respond differently or to use our previous experiences of this path to encourage fellow travellers who are walking it for the first time.

Pray

Dip the marble into the paint, then add it into the tray on top of your paper. Tilt the tray at different angles and watch as the marble rolls around, leaving a path of paint. The marble may go unexpected ways and go back over areas it had already covered with a pathway of colour. Pray as you watch the marble make a unique set of lines on the page. In life, even when the journey seems so messy and you are going over old ground, God is in control and there is a plan, a reason and a purpose to the path you are on. When you feel unable to walk, when the journey is hard and the challenges are many, when your faith is tested, God will carry you. The prayers and support of others can sustain and uphold you when you are greatly burdened or unsure how to keep going. Pray about all these as you watch the marble roll around, making a unique and intricate yet rather unexpected series of paths across the paper. There is beauty in the mess and God uses our repeated experiences to help us grow and be able to help others. Take your picture away with you, as a visual reminder of the many unexpected turns the path of life can take and the roads we sometimes retread, as well as of the fact that God yet carries us and we do not travel alone.

Walking in the footsteps of Jesus

Prayer focus

Not following our own paths but seeking wisdom to walk as Jesus walked, as we follow in his footsteps. To be an example to others, reflecting on the footprints we leave behind and the impact we can make for God.

Bible reflection

> Let your eyes look straight ahead; fix your gaze directly before you. Give careful thought to the paths for your feet and be steadfast in all your ways. Do not turn to the right or the left; keep your foot from evil.
>
> PROVERBS 4:25–27

What I need

- Long roll of plain paper
- Paint in various colours
- Plastic trays
- Washing-up bowls filled with bubble bath or washing-up liquid
- Towels (paper or towelling)
- Duct tape or masking tape
- Water
- Chairs

Tape to a suitable floor a long path of paper. Fill the trays with paint and washing-up bowls with bubbly warm water, placing these at opposite ends. Set out chairs and towels next to the bowls of water.

Reflect

Our faith calls us to walk in obedience with God, seeking his path for our life and to walk in his ways. It is easy to be distracted, to wander from the path. When we remain focused on God and walk in the footsteps of Jesus, we can make an eternal footprint on earth, an impact that is visible to those around us and that reflects our journey with God. It can take prayer to choose the right path, seeking God first in every step of our life journey. As Christians, we need to encourage each other on our faith journeys, joining people all over the world who are striving to walk in the ways of Jesus, to be his hands and feet on earth today. It takes perseverance, but God can help us to remain steadfast in our faith, as we follow the example of Christ, and to fulfil our part in the great commission to share God's love.

Pray

With bare feet, step into a tray of paint and walk a path of footprints along the paper pathway. Reflect as you do this, perhaps praying for God to guide your path and direct your steps of faith, as you seek to walk in the footsteps of Jesus. Pray for fresh strength to keep steadfast and focused in your faith, and to be obedient to his calling on your life, though the path may not be easy and you may grow weary at times. When you reach the end of the path, sit down and rest a while as you wash and dry your feet, taking time to give thanks for the journey of your faith so far and the way God gives you the strength you need to continue to walk in his ways. Look back at your footprints and those others have made. Use the sight of many sets of footprints to pray for those you walk alongside, that we might support and encourage each other to remain steadfast in our faith, when the journey is hard and we each follow the path God has for us. You have taken steps alongside the faithful in the world, and made a visual image of your walk with God and those who walk alongside you in your community. It is also a small reflection of the worldwide church that walks a journey of faith and seeks to take the great commission to all corners of the earth.

God with us in the valleys and heights

Prayer focus

To recognise that God is with us in every season of life, looking back at when he was most evidently there along your life journey and faith walk, whether in valley days or incredible heights of blessing.

Bible reflection

'Every valley shall be raised up, every mountain and hill made low; the rough ground shall become level, the rugged places a plain.'

ISAIAH 40:4

What I need

- A4 construction paper
- Scissors
- Glue sticks
- Pens or pencils (optional)

Cut out strips of paper. Leave plenty of uncut A4 sheets, too.

Reflect

Life is punctuated with seasons of struggle, when we travel through deep valleys of ill health, bereavement, uncertainty or spiritual wandering. In contrast, there are many joyful, uplifting experiences interwoven into our journey. When we choose to put our trust in God, he does not promise a straight, smooth path ahead. When we invite him to walk with us in every season, we can know comfort in even the deepest valley; where hope seems lost, he can lead us through. God can help us walk to heights we never felt achievable in our own strength, when we trust him to guide our steps. He can raise us up from the lowest of valleys and set us firmly on the rock of his love, higher than we could imagine possible. But we have to experience the valleys to appreciate the views when we ascend to the heights.

Pray

Cut strips of equal thickness along almost the full length of a piece of paper, stopping so you leave a decent solid margin at the end. Reflect on the different seasons of your life as you take some loose paper strips and begin to weave the first one through the strips you've just prepared. Start from the loose end of the paper, weaving it over and under, praying about the highs and lows of life, then slide this first strip along to meet the fixed end and begin another one. Take your time to weave the paper up to mountain height shapes and under into valleys below the fixed strips. If you started to weave the first one with an under action, start the next one by weaving it over the strip, weaving each strip in an alternating pattern. Continue to do this all the way along the paper as you meditate on the heights and valleys you have experienced in your life and faith, bringing them prayerfully to God. Give thanks as you think back on those valleys and heights God has already carried you through. Secure the end by gluing a strip vertically along the ends of all the horizontal strips of paper. Use this final step as a confirmation of all your prayerful meditation, trusting God to make your paths smooth. Close by asking God to keep you fixed on him in the valleys and heights, secure in him as your constant.

15
Names of Jesus

Who do you say I am?

Prayer focus

To use objects as visual prompts to inspire your reflections and guide your personal prayer on the names and identities of Jesus – king, healer, friend, shepherd, redeemer and more.

Bible reflection

> 'But what about you?' [Jesus] asked. 'Who do you say I am?' Simon Peter answered, 'You are the Messiah, the Son of the living God.'
> MATTHEW 16:15–16

What I need

- Objects to represent the names of Jesus – e.g. crown (lord/king), dove (prince of peace/Holy Spirit), wooden cross (redeemer), chalkboard (teacher), bandage/plaster (healer), heart (friend), small bottle of water (water of life). But get creative and use a variety of items
- Tray to lay the items out on, or bag to hold them all

Reflect

Jesus was known by many people as a healer, teacher and friend but he was also the fulfilment of prophecy and the hoped-for Saviour. When he asked his disciples who he was to them personally, Simon Peter's response showed he understood the significance of Jesus' identity as Messiah – not just a friend and a wise teacher, but also Immanuel (God with us), the embodiment of God's plan and the prophesied Saviour of the world. How would you respond if Jesus asked you the question, 'Who do you say I am?' Which of the biblical descriptions of Jesus do you most identify with, in the ways you have experienced Jesus in your faith journey? Who is Jesus to you today? Has this changed in different seasons of your life?

Pray

Take an object, chosen to represent elements of Jesus' personality or the roles he embodied in his life and ministry on earth and as part of God's plan. Reflect as you look at the object, hold it as you pray about your Jesus, who he is to you, inspired by the item. Use each item you choose to guide your prayers and spend time meditating on the symbolism of them, perhaps giving thanks for the times in your life and faith journey when you first knew Jesus as your redeemer, or when he healed or restored you. You may also want to think about other people in your life who have been significant in the way they have shown Jesus to you. This might be someone who, as a mentor, teacher or friend, played a part in your coming to faith. You may want to pray using each object in turn, or simply choose the ones you feel are most relevant to you and pray using these. When you are ready, commit your prayers to God, giving thanks to him for sending Jesus to be all the things you have reflected upon, then place the items back ready for someone else to use.

Jesus, my teacher

Prayer focus

To reflect on Jesus as teacher, a mentor and guide in our faith. To meditate on the words of truth and wisdom that he shared in his teaching ministry and the ways we can learn from him in our daily walk of faith.

Bible reflection

'You call me "Teacher" and "Lord", and rightly so, for that is what I am. Now that I, your Lord and Teacher, have washed your feet, you also should wash one another's feet. I have set you an example that you should do as I have done for you.'
JOHN 13:13–15

What I need

- Large chalkboard or series of small slates
- Chalks in various colours
- Eraser for chalkboard
- Bibles
- Paper
- Pens or pencils

Place the chalkboard or slates, chalks and eraser out. Put out the Bibles, paper and pens or pencils.

Reflect

Jesus spoke to large crowds or small gatherings of friends and imparted wisdom and knowledge. Though Jesus healed the sick and made known his identity as the Son of God, there are many accounts of him simply taking the time to sit with people or preach to those who had travelled to hear him speak. He told stories that powerfully taught Christian principles and reflected the mercy and love of his heavenly Father. Which of his parables or illustrations have had a significant impact on you in your understanding of God and your faith development? How does the teaching of Jesus inform the way you try to live your life?

Pray

Consider all you have learned from the teaching of Jesus, lessons for living that have shaped how you conduct yourself and speak of God to others. Using the Bibles provided, spend some time reading again some of the parables and teaching of Jesus. Perhaps choose a favourite story or one which you feel you need to read afresh. In taking some time looking through the gospels of Matthew, Mark, Luke and John, you might find some verses that you are unfamiliar with that speak to you today, as you prayerfully ask God to lead you in your reflections on the scriptures.

On the board or slate provided, write a verse that you have benefited from learning or inscribe a prayer of thanksgiving to Jesus, the teacher. If you would like to take home a reminder of the teaching of Jesus that you've been reflecting on, use the paper and pens or pencils provided to make a note of the Bible reference or write out a part of scripture or a short prayer.

Jesus, my friend

Prayer focus

To pause and reconnect with Jesus, your friend, over a cuppa. To have a chat with Jesus, in the same way you would confide in a friend or relative. To pray as you relax and pause to refresh. To spend time with your friend and Saviour.

Bible reflection

> 'I no longer call you servants, because a servant does not know his master's business. Instead, I have called you friends, for everything that I learned from my Father I have made known to you.'
>
> JOHN 15:15

What I need

- Cardboard
- Scissors
- Pens or printer
- Stapler
- Teabags or coffee in individual sachets
- Mugs or cups and saucers
- Tea- and coffee-making facilities, including milk and sugar

Set a table for tea, adding any little touches you like, e.g. flowers, tablecloth, biscuits. Cut out mug or teapot shapes with the verse reference 'John 15:15' or 'Enjoy a cuppa with Jesus' written or printed on them. Staple a coffee sachet or teabag (without piercing the contents) on to the corner of each one. Put these out.

Reflect

When we want to spend quality time with a friend, often we invite them around for a cuppa or arrange to meet for a coffee. We take time to listen to each other, pouring out our troubles to a trusted confidant, or update each other with our latest exciting news over a cup of our favourite brew. Jesus often shared food and drink with his closest friends and those who showed him hospitality on his preaching journey. He took time to sit, relax and chat. In the same way, although we cannot pour him a coffee or tea, why shouldn't we take time to pause and share a moment of peace and quiet with Jesus? Wouldn't you love to enjoy a cuppa in the presence of your friend and Saviour, as you tell him your cares and joys, listening to anything he wants to tell you? What would you tell him about?

Pray

Make yourself a cup of tea or coffee from the selection provided. Take time to be present in the experience; notice the smells and tastes. Focus fully on simply making a drink, imagining you are taking tea or having a coffee with Jesus. Let go of any other concerns or activities in these moments, having made this date to reconnect with your friend. Begin to pray by inviting Jesus to join you, to share in this time of relaxation and refreshment with you, to sit in companionable stillness together. Savour the drink; don't rush but devote some time to talking to Jesus through prayer, telling him anything that comes to mind, as you would in conversation with an intimate friend – he wants to hear about your worries or plans and recent activities. If you have never thought of your Lord and Saviour in this informal way, gently pray this through and ask that he might meet with you in this space.

Only when you feel ready, leave the table and take a cuppa card with you. Take time to pray each time you enjoy a cup of tea or coffee. You may want to give this to a friend or keep it to remind you to take time out to reconnect with Jesus when you drink a cuppa.

Jesus, my redeemer

Prayer focus

To reflect on the sacrifice of Jesus' crucifixion and the empty cross, a symbol of the power and redeeming love displayed for you and all humankind in his resurrection glory.

Bible reflection

> Our Redeemer – the Lord Almighty is his name – is the Holy One of Israel.
> ISAIAH 47:4

What I need

- Craft lollipop sticks
- Red wool or ribbon
- Scissors
- Glue gun or strong wood glue

Cut some long lengths of ribbon or wool. Glue the lollipop sticks together in cross shapes. Wrap red wool/ribbon around one of these crosses as a focal point for the station.

Reflect

To be redeemed is to be set free, to be fully won back, your debt paid in full. Through the sacrifice of pain that Jesus endured upon the cross, we can know him as our Saviour – he has redeemed us. Reflect on what redemption from sin means to you and all that the cross represents, as you look at the cross before you. Meditate on the way it is wrapped with red, to represent Jesus' blood shed for our transgression, paying the cost and setting us free. Consider the strips of material laid out, the stripes that Jesus bore willingly. See also that the cross is empty, representing his resurrection, which means we can live a life of freedom.

Pray

Take a cross shape in your hands, and reflect on the way we are redeemed by grace – Jesus made it possible for us to experience new life and live in relationship with God. Pray as you wind the material around the point where the lollipop sticks intersect to make a cross. Bring to your redeemer your prayers of thanksgiving for this most incredible gift, the ultimate sacrifice, as you secure the ribbon or wool by tying the ends. Meditate upon the image of a cross you have created, a representation of the sacrifice Jesus made for you. Lay your burdens at the cross in prayer, your worries and the things that come between you and God, acknowledging any ways you have sinned or wronged others in your words or deeds. Know that when you confess with a repentant and honest heart, your failings are forgiven. The cross you have made is empty! Though it represents Jesus' sacrificial death, it also reminds us that the cross was not the end of the story: death did not win. Jesus rose again in resurrected glory, fulfilling God's redemption plan. Take your cross away with you as a reminder of the redeeming love of Jesus.

16
Thanksgiving for God's provision

Jar full of joy

Prayer focus

To give thanks to God for the many positive experiences in our life. To reflect on the joys that fill our life and to use the remembrance of them to encourage us when we go through difficult times.

Bible reflection

'Do not grieve, for the joy of the Lord is your strength.'
NEHEMIAH 8:10

What I need

- Jars with lids (bought or washed-out jam jars)
- Slips of paper
- Scissors
- Address label stickers
- Pens
- Other decorations, e.g. stickers, glass pens, ribbon (optional)

Reflect

Often, our lives become filled with cares, stress and the busy demands of the everyday. We can forget to take time to appreciate the many joys life brings. If you could place all your happiest memories into a jar, preserving them and keeping them safe to look back on in difficult times, what would it contain? What joys has God blessed your life with? What are some of your most treasured memories? God wants us to know joy and peace and to be filled with his Holy Spirit so that we cannot help but rejoice in our blessings, whatever circumstances we face.

Pray

Take an empty jar and some slips of paper. Take some time to think on the joys in your life, the moments that have made you smile or brought you closer to God. On one of the slips, write a short sentence detailing a memory you cherish or an event that is particularly joyful for you. When you have written it, place the slip inside the empty jar. Reflect on prayers answered, unexpected blessings and significant times of deep joy and peace in your life. Write these down, each on a separate slip. Pray a prayer of thanksgiving for the blessing of joy as you place each one into the jar. You might want to add a label to the outside of the jar, perhaps with your name and 'my joys' or 'jar of joys' written on it, and to decorate the jar with stickers and tie a ribbon in a small bow around the neck, just below where the lid goes on.

This is your prayer response to take home. Be encouraged by the joys you have called to mind. Why not continue to add more slips at other times; you might want to date these. Use the jar as a symbol of how blessed with joy and hope you are. You can open the jar and select a paper to read in times of worry or upset, as a reminder of all the good things God has given you. You might like to empty out the jar at the end of the year, reading your collection of joys and reminiscing on all the moments of happiness you have experienced. Give thanks to God for the joy he fills you with and ask him to help you know fresh joy if you are going through a season of difficulty and need the strength and peace he can provide.

Taste and see that the Lord is good

Prayer focus

To reflect on God's goodness, the nourishment he provides that fulfils our physical and spiritual needs. To thank God for his provision for us and for his love that sustains us.

Bible reflection

Taste and see that the Lord is good; blessed is the one who takes refuge in him.
PSALM 34:8

What I need

- Ceramic plates
- Ceramic paint or pens
- Varnish (optional)
- Sweet fruit, or other selection of sweet foods

Reflect

In using the words 'taste' and 'see' in the verse from Psalm 34, the psalmist is inviting us not just to know in our minds that God is good and can provide for our every need but also to experience personally the benevolence of God: to savour his goodness like a delicious food, not an abstract concept but a sensory experience. We can be comforted by the goodness of God when we trust that he will provide for our every need. Have you 'tasted' God's goodness? Do you know its sweetness and the way it can satisfy your every hunger, like a delicacy that delights our senses and leaves us satisfied?

Pray

Take a plate. Use the ceramic pens or paints to decorate it, praying as you do this. You might want to add drawings of your favourite food or foods you find particularly tasty. You could write the verse from Psalm 34 on the plate, a prayer of thanksgiving or words to represent the way God fulfils our needs and nourishes us physically and spiritually. Enjoy some food as you pray, and take time to really experience the sweetness of it, as you give thanks to God for the ways he provides for you – the times you have experienced a taste of his goodness and demonstrations of his love in your life. You might want to ask God for a fresh sense of this, to really taste or encounter God's goodness with your senses, not just to know that he is good. Take your plate home to display as a reminder of God's goodness or varnish it and use it.

Attitude of gratitude

Prayer focus

To write a prayer in the form of a thank-you letter to God.

Bible reflection

> I will give thanks to you, Lord, with all my heart; I will tell of all your wonderful deeds.
> PSALM 9:1

What I need

- Writing paper or notecards and envelopes
- Pens in various colours

Reflect

In our age of instant communication, letter-writing is not something we do often. Is your prayer life sometimes like modern communication methods? Do you send God a quick prayer of thanks fired off like a text message? Perhaps you mean to give thanks to God but, like an unanswered text or email, you don't get around to it and the moment passes. If you could write a letter to God, what would it say? Receiving a letter from someone can be such a joy and, when someone takes the time to write and thank us for something we have done, it is so appreciated. Imagine how delighted God would be to receive your prayers of thanks, in a heartfelt letter of gratitude and thanksgiving, penned by his precious child.

Pray

Spend some time writing a letter or card to God. This may feel quite daunting; you might be unsure where to start or how to say the things you want to communicate to God. Pray before you put pen to paper, asking him to release you from any feelings of worry or uncertainty and to enable you to write your message of thanksgiving from the heart. Your letter is for God; don't be concerned with how it sounds or whether they are the right words. Simply write it in any style you feel, knowing that you are writing to your Lord, who loves to hear from you. The length of the letter is entirely up to you, a short note or a longer communication. Include anything you want to thank him for, the people and opportunities you are grateful for. You may also want to take the chance to pour out your love for God in the letter or apologise that you are not in touch as often as you used to be. When you are finished, sign it in a way that expresses your affection for God, as you would a letter to a loved one. Place it into an envelope, as a symbol of sending your letter to God. The Lord knows every thought and word before you speak it and will have read your words and received your prayers of thanksgiving. Take your letter with you as a reminder that you can communicate with God anytime and to encourage you to write again. Add further letters to God or perhaps just use the letter as a visual prompt to pause and pray – God is always listening and waiting to hear from you.

God fills our empty jars

Prayer focus

God provides and we can trust that he will meet our needs, even when times seem very bleak. To trust God to sustain us.

Bible reflection

'For this is what the Lord, the God of Israel, says: "The jar of flour will not be used up and the jug of oil will not run dry until the day the Lord sends rain on the land."'… For the jar of flour was not used up and the jug of oil did not run dry, in keeping with the word of the Lord spoken by Elijah.

1 KINGS 17:14, 16

What I need

- Small glass jam jars
- Oil
- Flour
- Address label stickers

Reflect

Sometimes situations in life can become very bleak: not just a little difficult but seemingly impossible to overcome. A family relationship broken, declining health or financial dire straits can leave us with little hope of any way back to restoration and wholeness, barring a miracle. But God can provide, however extreme our circumstance, and he can help us through, giving us the provisions we need. Complete restoration may not come, but when we trust God he will fill us with the strength we need and sustain us when we feel every ounce of our human strength and capacity to survive has dwindled.

Pray

In the story of the widow in 1 Kings, the Bible gives us an example of the Lord bringing hope and provision. In what ways do you need God to keep your jars full? Do you need to know a fresh outpouring of the oil of his love and strength to try again to restore a fragmented family connection? Or do you have practical needs that are concerning you, causing you to wonder how you can survive day by day, month on month, with the current state of your physical or mental health or finances stretched to the limit?

Take some time to open your heart to God. Share with him in prayer your worries and the things in life that feel empty, poured out and desolate. Select a small jar and fill it with some flour or oil, as your response to God, praying that he would fill you with a fresh anointing of the oil and salve of his love, wherever you need it in your life. Trust that he can provide a way forward. Give thanks for his provision and the ways he has sent just what you needed in the past to sustain and uplift you. Seal the jar as you close your prayer. You may want to write a prayer, part of the verse from 1 Kings or simply the words 'God fills our jars' on to a sticky label and add this to the jar. Take your jar away as a reminder to trust God to provide and give thanks for all he gives us.

Reflecting on our personal walk with God

17
Opening our hearts to God

Pouring out our hearts

Prayer focus

To pour out our hearts, hopes, failings and feelings to God. To pray for the courage to spread God's love around like the scattering of confetti. To pray that our words and actions might decorate the places we go with a sense of God's love.

Bible reflection

> Trust in him at all times, you people; pour out your hearts to him, for God is our refuge.
> PSALM 62:8

What I need

- Heart-shaped confetti, made from foil or colourful paper
- Paper/plastic cups or small glass jars
- Table cloth
- Tray (optional)

Fill the cups or jars with some confetti and place these out on a covered table.

Reflect

Our prayers sometimes take the form of pouring out our heart to God, just as we would to a friend or loved one. We can freely share with God, unburdening ourselves of those things that weigh heavily on our heart or talking about the things that we are bursting with excitement to share, with a thankful heart. Our hearts can also become filled with concerns for others. Our hearts go out to those in our wider community and the world who are suffering and in need. Jesus willingly poured out his love for us and his anguish for the suffering and sins of the world when he shed his blood upon the cross. This was the ultimate outpouring of love for a broken world, demonstrated by a blameless Saviour.

Pray

Take a container of heart-shaped confetti. Look at the hearts and reflect on the great love poured out by Jesus, when he shed his blood as a sacrifice for the sins of the world, so that we might know God's love. Bring to God all the concerns, hopes and joys that fill your heart, for yourself, your loved ones and the world. When you are ready, pour the confetti out and use this as a symbol of you giving to God all that is in your heart, your doubts, fears and delight. Pray that you might have opportunities to scatter God's love wherever you go, like confetti, that his love might be known. Take home a few little hearts as a reminder of your prayer. Use these to prompt you regularly to share all that is on your heart with God, or you may want to give some to others as you share with them about God's love.

Prayer for the broken-hearted

Prayer focus

To pray for those who are in need of healing from heartbreak. To bring our broken lives to God, trusting that he can bring new hope and wholeness.

Bible reflection

> He heals the broken-hearted and binds up their wounds.
> PSALM 147:3

What I need

- Pink or red A4 paper or card
- Pens or pencils
- Scissors

Cut out hearts, dividing each one down the middle in a zig-zag pattern, to create a series of broken hearts. Place these out in pairs, with a small gap between the two halves, and cut some whole hearts with the word 'God' written or printed on each one.

Reflect

There are many references to the heart in scripture. The psalms speak often of God being close to those who are crushed in spirit, whose hearts cry out to him. The Lord can bring healing and wholeness to those who are deeply hurt, spiritually and emotionally. God cares about every aspect of our lives. His heart breaks for those in need and he longs to heal our hearts. We in turn are called to love others with our whole heart and to act with love and compassion to those who are broken-hearted, sharing God's heart of love for the world.

Pray

On one half of a broken heart, write a prayer for those for whom your heart breaks: in your family, community or world, or you may want to write a prayer for yourself if you feel your heart has been hurt or broken, or is weary. Once you have done this, ask God to bring healing to hurts and to bind up the broken-hearted. As you pray, join the broken heart with its other half. When you have joined the pieces together, you might want to write 'God' or 'Lord' on the other half, as a symbol that you are trusting that God can heal the broken. Leave the heart joined as you commit your prayers to God. Take away a whole heart with the word 'God' on it as a reminder that God can heal our hearts with his amazing love, and to remind you to continue to pray to give your heart and the heartbreak of those you have prayed for to God.

His banner over me is love

Prayer focus

To know that God champions you and delights in declaring his love for you. To pray for confidence in his encouraging presence as God stands with you in every battle you face.

Bible reflection

> Let him lead me to the banquet hall, and let his banner over me be love.
> SONG OF SONGS 2:4

What I need

- Various material or paper in different colours or patterns
- Pink or pale red material or paper
- Scissors
- Fabric pens or felt-tip pens
- Long length of ribbon
- Sticky tape or glue
- Hole punch
- Sewing needle and thread (optional)

Cut out large bunting triangles from the coloured or patterned material, and hearts from the red or pink material or paper that will fit centrally on each bunting flag. Glue or sew one on to each bunting flag. Put these out along with the fabric pens or felt-tip pens and the ribbon.

Reflect

God's love is greater than any battle we may be facing in our life. It is stronger and more steadfast than any human love we will ever experience and has an eternal faithfulness that is difficult to comprehend. God declares his love for you with all the passion of a champion stating their devoted allegiance to the one they fight for. Banners are used in battle to encourage and rally the troops' confidence and to show clearly to the approaching enemy the cause or side for which the soldiers are willing to risk their all. We can be confident that God's love is everlasting. He will not retreat when the battle is long or the enemies that come against us are numerous. He has placed his banner of love over you and declares his unfailing love for all to see. He celebrates your turning to him and will advocate for you and be the strength and presence you need, by your side in every difficulty you face.

Pray

Choose a triangle of bunting. Reflect on the heart at its centre, a symbol of the love God has for you: a love that is above all things, stronger than death and more permanent than any other love you can experience. Write a prayer on to the bunting. Meditate on God's love for you as you decorate your bunting 'banner' with words, pictures or a whole prayer, either in the heart or around it on the flag. Alternatively, you may simply want to write your name within the heart as you consider the faithfulness of God and his devotion to you.

Punch a hole at the top corners of your flag and add it on to the ribbon as your response to God, acknowledging that you want to show your love for God and celebrate the love he has shown you. Give thanks, as you finish adding your part of this banner, for God's presence in your life, championing your cause and fighting for you. Display the bunting as a visual reminder that God's love is over everything, and his banner over each of us is love.

Fizzing over with love

Prayer focus

To reflect on the love God demonstrated in sending his son to be the ultimate sacrifice for us. To share with others the incredible news of Jesus' victory over death that brings us eternal life.

Bible reflection

> For God so loved the world that he gave his one and only Son, that whoever believes in him shall not perish but have eternal life.
> JOHN 3:16

What I need

- Mini tubes of fizzy heart sweets
- Cardboard
- Printer or pens
- Bowls
- Sticky tape
- Scissors

Produce verse cards with the words of John 3:16 printed or written on them and with room above to stick a tube of fizzy heart sweets. Put out bowls filled with loose fizzy heart sweets and some with the cards with sweets attached.

Reflect

Consider God's amazing heart for humanity that he sent Jesus to die and rise in resurrected glory, so that you could live life to the full and know the love of God. Do you still fizz with joy and excitement when you think about the love God has for you? In any relationship, those first sweet, fizzing-over emotions can wear off with time. Yet the love you experienced in first discovering Jesus as your Saviour is as real today as it ever was. However long you have been journeying in your faith, God remains steadfast and his passionate love for you has not diminished. Read the well-known verse from John 3:16 again as you reflect on the incredible love that sent Jesus to the cross, sacrificed so that we might live in freedom from sin and know everlasting life.

Pray

Eat a fizzy heart, and consider the way it fizzes on your tongue. Remember how your heart fizzed with excitement when you first encountered Jesus. While you eat some more sweets, reflect on what this verse means for you personally, whatever stage you are at in your journey with God. Do you need to pray for a renewal of the passion and sweetness you once experienced in your relationship with God? Perhaps you want to give thanks for his love that has continued to impact your life as you have grown in your faith. Take the opportunity to share God's love with others! Take a verse card home with a little tube of the fizzy heart sweets taped to it and give it away to someone – pray that as they enjoy the sweets, they might reflect on the love of God.

18
Bringing our emotions to God

Things that make you smile

Prayer focus

To share with God our feelings of upset or worry, asking him to help us replace these emotions with happiness. To give thanks for our blessings – the things that make us smile.

Bible reflection

'So with you: now is your time of grief, but I will see you again and you will rejoice, and no one will take away your joy.'
JOHN 16:22

What I need

- Paper plates
- Pens
- Pencils
- Erasers
- Googly eyes
- Glue
- Wool or pipe cleaners (optional)

Reflect

There are many things in life that make us smile – happy memories, time spent with friends or family and recollections of significant times in our faith journey. Life also brings many challenges, changes and events that cause us to feel far from joyful, when even mustering a smile is so very difficult. However you are feeling today, take some time to consider the joys you have in your life and the moments that made you beam with happiness. Think back on the blessings you have known, even if the current season of your life is troubled and raising a smile takes huge effort because your heart is heavy with cares.

Pray

Select a paper plate, add googly eyes and draw facial features, using the pens provided, leaving a blank space for the mouth. If you have time, you can use the wool or paper cleaners to add hair. While you do this, reflect on those things that concern you, the things that take away your joy or make it hard to smile some days. With a pencil draw a frown, a downturned smile for the mouth. Prayerfully lay these emotional burdens of sadness or worry before God, asking him to help you overcome them and to smile once more. Trust that God can bring peace when you share your heartache with him. In response, take an eraser and rub out the downturned smile and replace it with a happy smile, drawn in felt-tip pen this time! Even if you don't feel this way right now, pray and trust that God can bring hope and joy even in the saddest times and that you will smile again. If you feel happy, use this as a time to give thanks in prayer for all the things that make you smile. We have so much to be thankful for! Ask God to fill you with feelings of happiness as you take away your face, with the frown replaced with a smile, thanking God for your blessings and leaving your worries with him.

Bursting with anger

Prayer focus

To release negative feelings of anger or upset, bring these emotions to God in prayer and ask for his help to let them go.

Bible reflection

> But now you must also rid yourselves of all such things as these: anger, rage, malice, slander, and filthy language from your lips.
> COLOSSIANS 3:8

What I need

- Red, green and blue uninflated balloons
- Pins

Put out several balloons of each colour and some pins.

Reflect

Emotions like anger, jealousy or deep sadness can build up inside us and have a hugely negative effect on our well-being and the way we behave towards others, if they go unaddressed. Do you keep feelings of jealousy or anger to yourself, rather than talking them through with someone you trust? Meditate on any feelings that you may be carrying, perhaps even without realising they have stayed with you. It can be hard to admit to having feelings of anger or jealousy or to be vulnerable and share how deeply a bereavement or sad event has filled our heart and mind.

Pray

Take a balloon in the colour representing the emotion you want God to help you let go of, with red symbolising anger, green jealousy and blue sadness. Blow the balloon up and, as you do this, use the action of your breath filling the balloon as a prayer. As your breath fills the balloon, imagine you are exhaling the feelings of anger, jealousy or sadness. When the balloon is full, tie its end closed. Hold the balloon for a few minutes, naming the emotions you have filled the balloon with before God, asking him to help you let them go. Relinquish their power over you, asking the Lord to help you continue to give them into his care when they threaten to overwhelm you again. Then, to symbolise your determination to not let these feelings have control in your life, burst the balloon with a pin. If you feel you need to deal with other emotions, select a balloon of another colour and repeat the prayer. Take a coloured balloon away with you, to repeat this prayer again when you need to.

God sees every teardrop

Prayer focus

To bring our upset and sadness to God. To know that it's okay to cry. God can heal our hurts and bring hope where there is sadness or loss.

Bible reflection

> You keep track of all my sorrows. You have collected all my tears in your bottle. You have recorded each one in your book. My enemies will retreat when I call to you for help. This I know: God is on my side!
>
> PSALM 56:8–9 (NLT)

What I need

- Large sheet of plain cardboard
- Marker pen and felt-tip pens
- Blue tissue paper
- Scissors
- Adhesive putty (e.g. BluTack)
- Cloth handkerchief

Draw a large head and neck outline on the cardboard. Use the marker pen and felt-tip pens to add features, leaving room to add tissue-paper teardrops to the face. Cut tissue-paper teardrops in proportion to the eyes and face. Fix these on to the face with adhesive putty and put an open handkerchief nearby.

Reflect

Crying is a natural expression of many emotions, including grief, joy, anger and hurt. It is sometimes seen as a sign of weakness, yet it is a normal, healthy way of expressing feelings and there is no shame in needing to cry sometimes, to release your emotions. There are many references to tears and weeping in the Bible, people experiencing deep anguish and crying out to God in prayer to express their turmoil when words don't come easily. Have you ever cried out to the Lord in prayer when you couldn't put your feelings into words? Or felt so full of joy as you let go of something or gave thanks to God that happy tears poured down your face?

Pray

Look at the paper teardrops on the face, and begin to gently open up to God about any feelings of upset, anger or joy that this image of weeping brings to mind. These might be emotions you are dealing with now or a memory of a time of sorrow or when you cried out to God. When you are ready, take a teardrop from the face and hold it in your hands as you meditate. You might want to think of times when God helped you overcome a particularly sad or difficult time in your life and replaced your tears of anguish with peace. Or you might want to pour out to God something that is heavy on your heart right now. He knows every emotion and sees every tear you cry; he knows the times when you have wept with deep hurt or overwhelming joy, each teardrop like a prayer words cannot express. Do not worry if you find that you cry as an expression of the raw emotions you might be experiencing as you do this prayer. Seek someone to pray with you if you need support today. In response, as you close your prayer, take a tissue teardrop, screw it up and place it on the handkerchief as a symbol of God drying our tears and replacing them with feelings of hope and joy.

Tapestry of emotions

Prayer focus

To bring all our emotions to God, trusting he knows the full picture of our life, not the tangled muddle of experiences on our journey.

Bible reflection

> For we are God's handiwork, created in Christ Jesus to do good works, which God prepared in advance for us to do.
> EPHESIANS 2:10

What I need

- Lollipop sticks
- PVA glue
- Red, blue, yellow and green wool
- Scissors
- Glue gun or strong wood glue

Cut some lengths of each colour of wool. Glue four lollipop sticks together in a square frame. Prepare enough of these squares in advance for your group.

Reflect

Our lives are like a tapestry, a complex weaving together of experiences, made up of seasons of contrasting emotions. We are God's handiwork! If we only trust his skilled hand, he will bring beauty from the seemingly jumbled mess of our life. Sometimes we can wonder what the Lord can possibly do with the tangled web of our days. We see only a mixture of threads of changeable emotions and experiences, but God sees the picture that is revealed on completion – he knows the plans and purpose for our life.

Pray

Take a square lollipop-stick frame and choose a colour of wool to begin your response, praying to God about the various emotions that make up the tapestry of our life's journey. Use yellow to represent happy times and blue for times of sadness or upset; red symbolises times when you felt angry and green represents jealousy or envious feelings. Tie the end of a piece of wool to any point around the frame and begin to weave it randomly around the frame side to side, crossing over in a woven pattern, as you ask God to help you understand his plan for your life, the learning and growing you can do through the experiences you feel led to reflect upon during this activity. Use different colours and pray about each emotion and the way it has made up part of the intertwined experiences in your life and faith journey.

God knows and loves you, and he will one day reveal the full, beautiful picture of your life. You will then see that every thread that God weaved into your life's path was needed, the ones that shine with bright colour and those that were dark. When you are focusing on difficult emotions like anger or sadness, use the verse from Ephesians to remind you that God has a plan and a purpose for you and can help you deal with these. You can reflect Christ, however haphazard your tapestry of emotions – you are God's masterpiece. Keep your tapestry as a reminder to trust that God has a plan and to help you accept or learn from your many differing emotions, which are all part of the picture of who God made you to be.

19
Sharing our worries with God

Hanging our worries out to dry

Prayer focus

To let go of our concerns about everyday tasks or our material needs, giving our worries to God in prayer, trusting he will provide.

Bible reflection

> 'And why do you worry about clothes? See how the flowers of the field grow. They do not labour or spin… If that is how God clothes the grass of the field, which is here today and tomorrow is thrown into the fire, will he not much more clothe you – you of little faith?'
>
> MATTHEW 6:28, 30

What I need

- Various coloured or patterned cardboard or material
- Washing line
- Pegs
- Pens
- Scissors

Put the washing line up. Cut out clothing outline shapes from the cardboard or material (e.g. trousers, dresses, T-shirts, socks).

Reflect

The teaching in these verses from Matthew gives a very clear message about ensuring we get our priorities right, not spending unnecessary time toiling and worrying. We cannot avoid having responsibilities, at home or at work, and caring about being well turned out is not a negative thing, but God does not want us to worry about these excessively. These verses challenge us to reassess what is truly important, to relinquish our human tendency to focus on how we look or what other people think, and to simply enjoy the blessings we have. We can learn from nature and stop setting such store on being busy and worrying about our appearance or how we will come by all the things we need, when we should be trusting God as our provider. Our creator, who took such care to clothe each flower with such delicate beauty, loves us so much that he will meet our needs, and he wants us to give all our worries into his care.

Pray

Choose an item of clothing from the shapes and bring to God in prayer the things that worry you and the times you work so hard, yet forget to pause and just trust him. Write these down on the garment shape as a prayer or a list of concerns. The God who clothed each flower in beautiful colours and cares about every single blade of grass is concerned about all the things that you need. Peg the item of clothing to the washing line as you give your worries to him. Hanging out the clothes not only reflects one of the many tasks we toil away at in daily life, but also symbolises us giving over to God our worries about our basic human necessities of clothing, food and shelter. Ask God to forgive you when you place too much importance on material things or become so busy you forget simply to trust that he can provide. Resolve to try to let go of concerns about where these provisions will come from. Let your faith be bigger than your worries; hang them out to dry, leaving them pegged where they are as you drop them in God's hands.

Your name is written on his hand

Prayer focus

To be secure in your identity in Christ. To know that you are precious to him and he knows your every worry and wants to carry your burdens.

Bible reflection

'See, I have written your name on the palms of my hands.'
ISAIAH 49:16 (NLT)

What I need

- Large sheet of cardboard
- Marker pens
- Pens of various colours
- Printer (optional)
- Paper in various colours
- Scissors

Draw or print a large outline of open hands, laid flat palms upwards, on the large piece of cardboard. Cut out a series of smaller hand shapes from the paper, and write or print the words of Isaiah 49:16, together with the words 'God knows your name. He knows you and loves you.'

Reflect

Your heavenly Father knows your name, the kind of person you are and the kind of person you want to be. He knows every hope, failing and worry. Whatever you think of yourself, or have been told by others, God knows the real you. Your creator knows you inside and out; your name is written on his hand and your identity is secure in him. Because of this, you can know peace, even when you feel overwhelmed with worries. Whatever life brings, God loves you with an everlasting love. Take some time to reflect on this truth and choose a hand with the verse from Isaiah printed on it. Read the words and reflect on them. God knows you and loves you; you are his precious child.

Pray

Take some time to absorb the knowledge of how loved you are, that God understands every worry and accepts you. Write your name on the large hands as your prayer response, as you acknowledge that you are so very important to God and your identity is secure in him. Draw or write a prayer on the reverse of your small paper hand if you wish and take this home with you as a reminder that you are known and loved by the creator of the world and that he wants you to place all your cares into his hands.

Box full of worries

Prayer focus

To trust our worries to God and leave them with him, letting go of control and not trying to sort them out ourselves.

Bible reflection

Give all your worries and cares to God, for he cares about you.
1 PETER 5:7 (NLT)

What I need

- Small gift boxes with lids
- Sticky tape
- Scissors/craft knife
- Paper
- Pens
- Stickers and felt-tip pens (optional)

Prepare the boxes by cutting a slot into the top, large enough to post small slips of folded paper through. Seal each box tightly closed by taping the lid to the base. Cut out strips of paper and put these out with the boxes and pens.

Reflect

Worry can multiply and take root as it plays over and again in our mind. It disturbs our peace and, however much we try to find a solution by ourselves, sometimes this only makes matters worse. Do you ever pray about a problem, only to then tie yourself in knots attempting to solve it in your strength and forget simply to leave it to God? It is rather like putting something broken in a box, placing it on a shelf, ready for someone with the right skills to mend it for you. But rather than letting them help you, you take the box back off the shelf, hoping somehow to work out how to bring restoration yourself. In holding on to it, no one can help fix the problem for you. God wants you to give your concerns to him, to let him remove the hold they have over you, releasing your mind from the weight of worry that you cannot lift by yourself. Are there things you are holding on to that you know you need to stop ruminating over – and give them completely to God?

Pray

Take a worry box and some slips of paper and a pen. Think about those things that concern you. Lay your worries down by writing them on the slips provided. You can either put just a word or two or write a longer description, but as you do this be confident that God knows every worry and wants to release you from the burden of the cares you carry. While you are writing, pray about the things that trouble you and, after writing each slip, fold the paper and post it into your box, placing your worries into God's care. It is very difficult to resist the urge to pick our problems back up and try to solve them ourselves. But they are now sealed in the box – you cannot take them back out! You have given them over to God in prayer. Take your box with you as a reminder to let God take over when you feel tempted to try to take those worries back. You can also add more worries to the box when you need to repeat the prayer process and continue to surrender your worries into God's hands.

Stamping out our worries

Prayer focus

To stamp out our worry, releasing our anxieties through a practical prayer response as an act of letting go and giving them over to God.

Bible reflection

> 'Therefore do not worry about tomorrow, for tomorrow will worry about itself. Each day has enough trouble of its own.'
> MATTHEW 6:34

What I need

- Large sheets of bubble wrap
- Scissors
- Masking tape or duct tape (optional)

Lay lots of bubble wrap on a suitable floor or table. If you are using the floor, you may want to tape it down to avoid anyone slipping. Cut some smaller squares of bubble wrap (no bigger than your palm) and put these out.

Reflect

How often do we add to our burden of cares, carrying worry with us rather than releasing it into God's hands? Each new day has its own challenges and worries – what if today you chose to stamp out the concerns that so occupy your thoughts? Look at the bubbles dotted all over the sheet of bubble wrap. Imagine for a moment that you could trap the things that weigh heavy on your mind inside those bubbles of air. They would then contain your worries, hurts and the things that you find difficult. As you meditate upon this, think of those things you would choose to encapsulate in the bubbles: the feelings of worry, hurt or anxiety that you would like God to help you 'stamp out' in your life, releasing you from carrying them any longer.

Pray

Give your worries over to God in prayer. Imagine those anxieties or concerns are now released from your mind and heart, and are held captive inside the bubbles of the bubble wrap. When you feel ready, begin to stamp on the bubble wrap sheet or pop a series of bubbles by hand. As you hear that therapeutic sound of each little bubble of air pop, take time to ask God to help you stamp out those worries you have prayed about, relinquishing them into his care. Take a small piece of bubble wrap with you, as a reminder of your prayer and for you to pop when you next start to feel the worry or anxiety trying to rob you of your joy and need to pray again.

20
Breaking the chains: prayers for freedom and forgiveness

Breaking chains that bind us

Prayer focus

To think about the freedom that Jesus has given us.

Bible reflection

It is for freedom that Christ has set us free. Stand firm, then, and do not let yourselves be burdened again by a yoke of slavery.
GALATIANS 5:1

What I need

- Grey paper, cut into strips
- Glue sticks
- Pens
- Small bin

Reflect

We all carry with us things that weigh us down and prevent us from truly walking in the freedom that God offers. Like a chain, forged link by link by each negative experience or our own behaviour, the heaviness of these can drag us down. When we carry each day the weight of bitterness towards others who have hurt us, it can prevent us from moving on and embracing the new life God has for us. Do you need God's help to break chains of unforgiveness or attitudes that you know you need to change? Are you shackled by fears or past experiences that stop you living life to the full? What holds you back from a life of freedom? God sent Jesus into the world to break the chains of sin and shame, giving us a clean start and a new lightness in our being, through his grace.

Pray

Begin to bring these things to God in prayer as you take a strip of paper. Write words or whole prayers along the strips of paper. They may describe behaviours or habits you know you need to change, fears and doubts, or past hurts – those things that prevent you from living life to the full or being all that God intended you to be. Take time to write three or four different strips. As you ask God to help you be free of these things, glue them together into a paper chain. Hold the chain in your hands as you pray. Offer to God those things that you know need breaking in your life, asking him to set you free from the things that bind you. As you close your prayers, break the chain apart and place the broken pieces into the bin, as a confirmation of your desire to live in freedom, to be all that God intended.

Clean start, clean heart

Prayer focus

God loves us despite our flaws and failings. To reflect on God's great love, which sees beyond our sin and imperfections and offers us freedom and a clean start.

Bible reflection

> But God demonstrates his own love for us in this: while we were still sinners, Christ died for us.
> ROMANS 5:8

What I need

- Slime (recipe available online) or jelly
- Bucket or large bowl
- Small plastic or wooden hearts (beads or similar)
- Wipes or bowl of hot soapy water
- Towel
- Waterproof table covering (or outdoor space, weather and venue permitting)

Make up in a bowl or bucket some slime or jelly in a suitably unappealing colour (e.g. green or brown). When it is a good gloopy consistency, add in the hearts, mixing them around so they are spread among the slime. Put out hand wipes or a bowl of hot soapy water and a towel.

Reflect

Jesus didn't die on the cross and rise in victory to redeem only those who are without sin or blemish. God loves us whatever state we are in, flawed and sinful – Jesus died for us all. However mature in our faith we are, we all fall short and fail, and we are all in need of grace. God meets us in the midst of our mess. He sent Jesus to give everyone the opportunity to have a fresh start: to know the freedom of being accepted, just as we are. God's mercy is found at the centre of even the most difficult things we go through. He doesn't wait for us to have everything figured out before he draws us into his loving embrace. He simply invites us, just as we are, to discover the treasure of his love for us. Through God's love, we can find freedom and a fresh start. However far we have wandered, whatever we have done, we can find forgiveness through Jesus. We can be washed clean and given a purified heart.

Pray

As you look at the repellent bowl of slime, meditate on those parts of you that are messy: the things you do or say that you know are wrong or the things that come between you and God. Within the unappealing gloopy mess, you might catch glimpses of something more attractive. Reach your hands in and take out one of the hearts that are enveloped by the mire. Take note of the state of the shape you have just retrieved and now also your own hands. Before you do anything else, use this unpleasant experience and image to guide your prayers, asking God to forgive the ways your hands or heart are blemished by sin and admitting to him the times you have messed up. Now wash the heart in the soapy water or wipe it down, as you ask God to wash you clean once more, wiping away all that has come between you and the love of God. Ask him to give you a fresh start, a clean heart. With your hands and the heart now washed clean, dry them and observe how both were cleansed of the slime that covered them, as you responded in prayer. Know that God can give you a new, clean heart. You can begin again and live in freedom, in the knowledge of his love for you. Take your heart with you as a reminder that God will always find you in the middle of the mire and has given you a clean heart to begin again.

Birds don't worry

Prayer focus

To respond in prayer by releasing a paper bird as a symbol of finding freedom by letting go of our worries and trusting God.

Bible reflection

> 'Look at the birds of the air: they neither sow nor reap nor gather into barns, and yet your heavenly Father feeds them. Are you not of more value than they?'
> MATTHEW 6:26 (ESV)

What I need

- A4 paper
- Felt-tip pens
- Stickers and other decorations (optional)

Reflect

Birds fly free, not concerning themselves with the kind of earthly things that we worry about. They trust the Lord to provide every need: the shelter they seek and the food they need to feed themselves and their young. They have no concept of material trappings, like clothes or other belongings; God has given them all the attire they require from birth, and they find their food and shelter in their natural surroundings. They fly without a thought for material wealth or possessions; God has already provided all they need. Are you held back from flying on wings of freedom, grounded by your worries about temporal or material concerns? Is God asking you to step out and trust him to help you fly in freedom, leaving behind your anxieties about the things that currently tether you?

Pray

Take a piece of A4 paper and fold it into a paper aeroplane bird. Relax and enjoy decorating this bird of prayer as you talk to God about your worries and ask him to reveal to you ways you can fly more freely, relinquishing concerns and focusing on the freedom he offers and the spiritual provision he clothes and feeds you with. Decorate, draw on or write on the bird as you pray – clothe it with words of prayer or write down all the worries you want to put to flight. When your creation is ready, hold it and prepare to release it, prayerfully confirming your desire to stop focusing on material needs and to place more trust in your creator. Watch as your paper bird freely flies without anything preventing it soaring in beautiful freedom. Ask God to show you ways you can embrace the same freedom from worry and accept the blessings he has for you. God can release us from worrying about things that are not important if we turn them over to him. We can be free to spread our wings, knowing that the God who clothes the birds of the air will provide all we need.

Let go, let God

Prayer focus

To find freedom through releasing our grip on our worries, allowing God to take control. To let go in order to let God be God, when we trust him with our concerns.

Bible reflection

> Let go of your concerns! Then you will know that I am God. I rule the nations. I rule the earth. The Lord of Armies is with us. The God of Jacob is our stronghold.
>
> PSALM 46:10–11 (GW)

What I need

- Biodegradable balloons of various colours, suitable for helium
- Helium canister
- Cardboard luggage tags with string
- Compostable curling gift ribbon
- Pens

Prepare some helium balloons in advance, blown up with a length of ribbon tied on. You will need to do the end of this prayer outside, though you may want to do the prayer writing indoors (to avoid helium balloons being released too soon).

Reflect

There is great freedom in letting go. Relinquishing our concerns to God in prayer can bring release from the things that weigh us down. Yet at times we hold on to worry, determined to resolve our own concerns, rather than asking for support. We underestimate God's power to set us free from our anxieties, however deep-rooted or ongoing. We may be ashamed of our feelings, embarrassed by the things that cause us to be downcast. Perhaps you feel you shouldn't bother God with such trivial matters as your worries, but God wants you to let go of your concerns. He already knows your every struggle and wants you to cast your burdens on him. In not letting go of every worry to our heavenly Father, we are not letting him be God over all aspects of our life. He wants to hear every prayer need from the anxious heart of his child and have the chance to show his strength and sovereignty.

Pray

Take a luggage tag and consider those worries that you struggle to give over to God, the areas of your life where you find it hard to let go of control or ask for help. Write a prayer on the tag or simply write the words 'let go' and 'let God'. Meditate, as you write these words, on the things you know you need to release to God, then consider what it truly means to let God be God. This involves trusting him with every part of yourself, letting him direct your life and allowing him into your heart in a way you may never have done before. Pray about this as you attach the tag and some ribbon to a helium balloon. When you are ready, commit your prayers and reflections to God as you release your balloon. Use this as your confirmation of letting go of control, acknowledging God's authority and trusting that he can help you overcome every worry when you let him be God. Watch as your balloon flies freely into the sky. Rejoice that whatever we are going through we can know freedom, when we let go and let God take our burdens.

Bible passage index

Prayer topic index

Resources index

Prayer is a vital part of the Christian life but people often struggle with actually getting on and doing it. This book offers 80 imaginative and creative ideas for setting up 'prayer stations', practical ways of praying that involve the senses - touching, tasting, smelling, seeing, and hearing, rather than simply reflecting, as we bring our hopes, fears, dreams and doubts to God.

80 Creative Prayer Ideas
A resource for church and group use
Claire Daniel
978 1 84101 688 7 £8.99

brf.org.uk

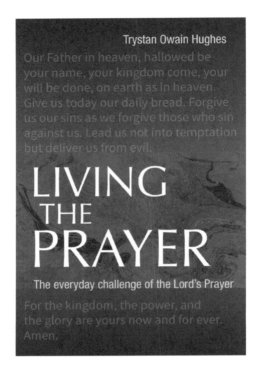

Living the Prayer is a fresh perspective on the Lord's Prayer. Rooted in the Bible as well as in contemporary culture, it explores how this prayer can radically challenge and transform our daily lives. Contained in the prayer's 70 words is a fresh and innovative way of viewing, and acting in, the world that is as relevant now as it was 2,000 years ago. The author shows that this revolutionary prayer demands that we don't remain on our knees, but, rather, that we work towards making God's topsy-turvy, downside-up kingdom an everyday reality.

Living the Prayer
The everyday challenge of the Lord's Prayer
Trystan Owain Hughes
978 0 85746 623 5 £7.99

brf.org.uk

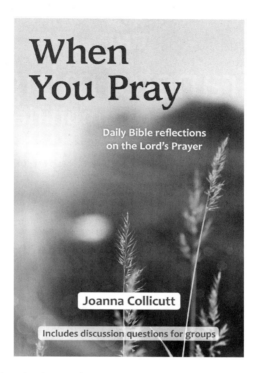

In this updated edition of a classic text, Joanna Collicutt shows how growing as a Christian is rooted in the prayer Jesus gave us. As we pray the Lord's Prayer, we express our relationship with God, absorb gospel values and are also motivated to live them out. As we pray to the Father, in union with the Son, through the power of the Spirit, so we begin to take on the character of Christ.

When You Pray
Daily Bible reflections on the Lord's Prayer
Joanna Collicutt
978 0 85746 867 3 £8.99

brf.org.uk

Transforming
lives and communities

Christian growth and understanding of the Bible

Resourcing individuals, groups and leaders in churches for their own spiritual journey and for their ministry

Church outreach in the local community

Offering two programmes that churches are embracing to great effect as they seek to engage with their local communities and transform lives

The Gift of Years

Teaching Christianity in primary schools

Working with children and teachers to explore Christianity creatively and confidently

Children's and family ministry

Working with churches and families to explore Christianity creatively and bring the Bible alive

parenting for faith

Visit **brf.org.uk** for more information on BRF's work

brf.org.uk

The Bible Reading Fellowship (BRF) is a Registered Charity (No. 233280)